la case books

THE TRUE STORIES OF THE MONSTER OF FLORENCE

JACOPO PEZZAN
& GIACOMO BRUNORO

THE TRUE STORIES
OF THE MONSTER OF FLORENCE
Jacopo Pezzan & Giacomo Brunoro
Copyright © 2025 LA CASE Books
Copyright © 2011 LA CASE Books
ISBN: 9781953546913
LA CASE Books PO BOX 931416, Los
Angeles, CA, 90093
info@lacasebooks.com
www.lacasebooks.com

CONTENTS

THE ENDLESS NIGHTMARE

This is the story of the most chilling and unsettling series of crimes to take place in Italy over the last forty years, a sequence of events that still echoes through the collective memory of the country. These crimes left behind not only fear, but also a deep sense of disorientation that has never been fully resolved. The story that follows is a puzzle, a disturbing mosaic for which we have an impressive number of pieces, perhaps even too many. Investigators, journalists, experts, and ordinary citizens have tried again and again to arrange those pieces into a coherent picture. Yet, no matter how hard we try to assemble them, they never seem to lock together in a way that provides a definitive truth.

This story is a bloody puzzle, a complex construction that reveals a terrifying image based on the fragments we choose, the ones we discard, and the ways we connect them. Every attempt at clarity leads instead to new shadows. Every theory opens the door to fresh contradictions. And no matter how the pieces are combined, the final picture always leads to too many open questions, too many unresolved threads, and too many moments where logic breaks down.

This is a story without a final word, a story suspended in uncertainty. For more than thirty years, it has inhabited the nightmares of one of Italy's most beautiful and internationally admired regions, Tuscany. Tourists know Tuscany for its rolling hills, its Renaissance heritage, its vineyards and ancient towns. But beneath that postcard beauty lies a darker layer of history, one that continues to disturb both locals and outsiders who have studied the case. The peaceful countryside and the romantic landscapes form a chilling contrast to the brutality that unfolded there.

What comes next is the storytelling of the crimes committed by the figure who came to be known as "The Monster of Florence". The mere phrase sends a shiver down the spine of anyone familiar with the case. It became the label that newspapers repeated, the nickname whispered in conversations, and eventually the symbol of a fear that spread far beyond the borders of Tuscany.

This was not simply a criminal investigation, not simply a hunt for a killer. It became a national obsession, a psychological labyrinth that challenged investigators and left entire communities anxious, confused, and desperate for clarity.

We are talking about an event that has tested every existing criminology theory on serial killers. Experts from Italy, Europe, and the United States have examined the case and attempted to categorize the murderer within known behavioral patterns. Yet each attempt has failed to capture the full complexity of what happened. The crimes demonstrated an unsettling combination of precision, ritual, and cruelty that did not fully align with any established profile. Over time, the case forced scholars to rethink assumptions about serial offenders and about how investigations should be conducted when the evidence seems to contradict itself.

To understand the impact of these crimes, it helps to think of criminology as divided into three levels. There are traditional crimes, driven by motives that investigators know well, such as passion, revenge, money, or impulse. Then there are serial killers, whose motives follow darker and more deviant paths but still tend to repeat recognizable behavioral patterns. And then there is "The Monster of Florence", a presence that stands apart, a case so unusual and so difficult to frame that it remains one of the most troubling mysteries in modern Italian history.

The story that follows is not only the account of murders. It is also the story of the investigations, the false leads, the theories constructed and dismantled, and the countless people whose lives were shaped by the search for the truth. The Monster of Florence is not a simple chapter in criminal history. It is a phenomenon that continues to raise questions about justice, about institutional failures, about the fragility of truth when confronted with fear, and about how a nation processes trauma when the answers remain forever out of reach.

THE CRIMES

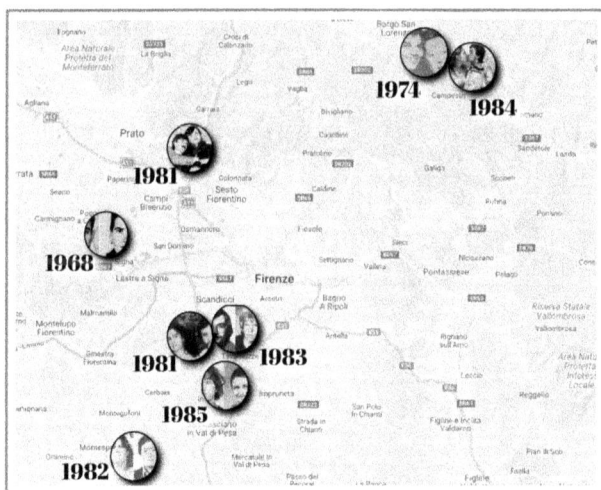

SATURDAY,
SEPTEMBER 14, 1974

Place: Borgo San Lorenzo, about 40
kilometers from Florence.

It is 9 pm when Pasquale Gentilcore arrives at
the Teen Club in Borgo San Lorenzo. He is
nineteen, works as a blue-collar employee, and
has given a ride to his sister, who plans to spend
the evening at the nightclub. Pasquale has already
agreed to return around midnight to pick her up.
His plan for the next few hours is simple. He
wants to drive to Pesciola di Vicchio to meet his
girlfriend, Stefania Pettini.

Stefania is eighteen and has started a new job
as a secretary with Magif of Florence. Pasquale
and Stefania have been together for two years.
Their relationship has grown in a steady and
natural way. Anyone who knew them described

them as a close couple with common plans and a quiet routine. On that evening, nothing suggests tension or trouble. Pasquale drives his blue FIAT 127, a car his father lent to him. The car has a radio, a detail that gave a sense of comfort in those years. He listens to music as he leaves the nightclub behind and heads toward Stefania's home.

Summer is ending, but the air still feels mild. It rained the night before, though the temperature is not cold. Pasquale drives through the area with a calm attitude. He enjoys the moment, the road, the music, and the idea of spending time with Stefania. His thoughts follow a simple path. Work, family, his relationship, and small plans for the evening.

It is around 9:30 pm when he stops in front of Stefania's house. She lives there with her family. She comes out, walks toward the FIAT 127, and gets inside the car. From that point forward, the known sequence ends. What happens after they drive away remains unknown, and the story enters a space without witnesses or clear answers.

Pasquale Gentilcore
and Stefania Pettini

Italian daily newspaper of
the time.

The lifeless body of Pasquale Gentilcore inside the car.

The lifeless body of Pasquale Gentilcore inside the car.

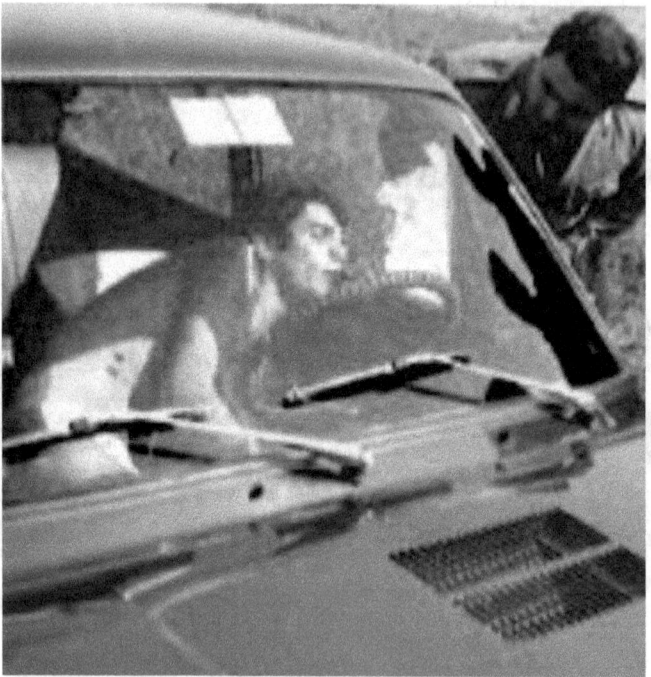

The lifeless body of Pasquale Gentilcore inside the car.

The lifeless body of Stefania Pettini.

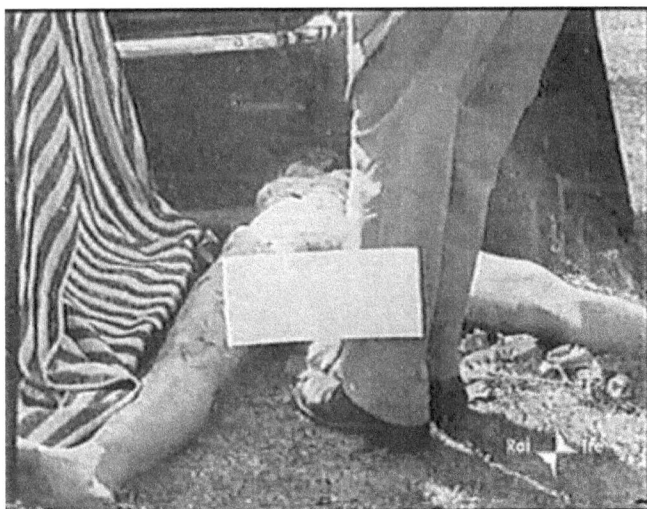

The lifeless body of Stefania Pettini.

SATURDAY, JUNE 6, 1981

Place: Mosciano di Scandicci, about 15 km
from Florence.

It is a moonless Saturday night, the kind of night in which darkness seems thicker than usual and silence carries farther than expected. Summer is nearing, and in the countryside around Florence the air has that warm softness typical of early June evenings. In the distance, the lights of the nightclub Anastasia glow faintly, a point of reference in an otherwise black landscape. The surrounding area is known to locals as a popular spot for couples seeking privacy and for the so-called "peeping toms" who move through the dark like shadows, hoping to glimpse fragments of other people's intimacy. It is a slice of Tuscan nightlife that exists away from restaurants, piazzas, and family gatherings. Hidden corners where people go to escape, to love, or to watch.

Inside a parked car, not far from the nightclub, two young people are spending what should have been an ordinary evening, one of many in their brief but promising relationship. The young man is Giovanni Foggi, thirty years old, a warehouse worker at ENEL, the national power company. Giovanni is described by those who knew him as responsible, quiet, and dedicated to his job. With his steady income and pragmatic mindset, he embodies the sort of stability many families valued in those years. Sitting next to him is Carmela De Nuccio, recently hired by the leather goods company ASI in Scandicci. She is young, with a bright future, and proud of her new job. She approaches this new stage of her life with enthusiasm, eager to prove herself in a field that has long been a pillar of the Florentine economy.

The two of them have been dating for only a few months, yet the relationship has advanced quickly and naturally. Their families are already aware that the couple has begun speaking openly about marriage. Giovanni and Carmela seem to move through their days with the certainty of two people who feel they have found the right partner. Earlier that evening, they had dinner at Carmela's house, sharing a meal with her parents. It was a calm, normal family dinner, without anything to hint at the tragedy that would unfold only a few hours later. After dinner they decided to leave for a short outing, planning to get some ice cream at around 10 pm. It was a typical Saturday plan, modest but pleasant, and perfectly in keeping with the routines of young couples in those years.

Yet while they enjoy those ordinary moments, the Monster is already moving through the night. The attack, when it comes, is swift and brutal, an assault executed with such precision that the victims barely have time to react. Giovanni is hit first, struck by three precisely delivered shots. One bullet pierces his heart, another lung, and a third strikes his head. The violence is instantaneous and lethal. Carmela is targeted next. She is hit with five shots, one fired at point-blank range into her upper body, causing a fatal wound. The entire attack lasts only seconds. The Monster's method displays familiarity with weapons, composure, and a terrifying form of efficiency.

The gun used once again is a Beretta caliber .22, and later ballistic examinations confirm that it is the same firearm employed in the 1974 murders. The ammunition is Winchester H series, an additional detail that links the attack to the earlier homicides with chilling clarity. Once the shots have been fired, the Monster opens the car door. He reaches for Carmela, pulls her from the vehicle, and carries her to an embankment approximately twelve meters away. There, her body is later found fully dressed, though in a haunting pose, her necklace clenched tightly between her teeth. This detail becomes one of the most disturbing and puzzling symbols of the entire incident and will be discussed for years to come.

What happens next goes far beyond murder. After cutting her jeans up to the belt, the Monster uses a knife to remove her pubis. This act marks the first in a series of mutilations that investigators will come to view as the killer's macabre, ritualistic signature. The ground surrounding her body shows no signs of dragging, suggesting that Carmela was carried to the embankment rather than pulled along the soil. The killer demonstrates control and physical strength, but also a kind of methodical calmness that contradicts the idea of a frenzied attack. Before leaving the scene, he opens Carmela's purse and scatters its contents on the ground. He then returns to Giovanni, stabbing the young man post-mortem as if to leave behind a final insult. Only after completing these actions does he disappear into the night.

The bodies are discovered the following day by a policeman taking a walk with his son. They come upon the horrific scene with the disbelief and confusion that accompany such encounters.

Giovanni's body remains inside the car. He sits slumped on the driver's seat, the window next to him shattered completely. His pants have been pulled halfway down, a detail that immediately inspires multiple theories. Some investigators initially interpret this as a sign that Giovanni was attacked while preparing for sexual activity, caught off guard in a moment of vulnerability. Others, however, point out that the position of the pants might suggest that he was getting dressed, not undressed. Giovanni's right leg is found almost completely slipped into his pants, a detail that aligns more closely with the theory that he was interrupted while putting his clothes back on.

This second interpretation becomes especially relevant given the absence of any evidence of consummated sexual intercourse. If Giovanni had been dressing rather than undressing, it might indicate that the couple was preparing to leave the area. Perhaps they had heard something. Perhaps they sensed someone approaching the car. Perhaps they saw a shadow in the darkness that made them nervous. Whatever the reason, something may have disturbed them shortly before the attack. This detail, seemingly small, becomes one of the many pieces in the massive puzzle that investigators will attempt to assemble over the years.

It is at this point that one of the most ambiguous and mysterious figures connected to the entire Monster of Florence case comes into the spotlight: Enzo Spalletti. Born in Montelupo Fiorentino in 1945, Spalletti lives in the same town at the time of the crime. He works as an ambulance driver for Misericordia, a local organization similar to the Red Cross. Spalletti is known in certain circles for his activities at night. He is a "peeping tom", or as they were known in local slang, an "indian". This term referred to the numerous individuals who spent their nights roaming the outskirts of Florence, hiding among bushes and wooded areas, seeking the thrill of spying on couples. It was a subculture few admitted to, but many participated in. A secret world hidden beneath the surface of ordinary life.

On the evening of June 6, Spalletti's car is spotted near the crime scene, and someone later reports this sighting to the authorities. That night, he had met a friend at the pizza parlor "Taverna del Diavolo" in Roveta. The two spent the late evening lurking in the dark, waiting for opportunities to spy on couples. Around midnight, the friend decided the evening had been unproductive, said goodbye to Spalletti, and went home. Spalletti, however, did not return home until around 2 am.

In the days that follow the homicide, Spalletti reveals something unsettling. He tells his wife, and later a couple of bar customers, that he witnessed a young couple being murdered. He even mentions the mutilations. The problem is that he speaks about details that had not yet been published in newspapers. The information he provides was not available to the public at the time he mentioned it. This fact alone turns him into a person of intense interest for investigators.

When detectives bring him in for questioning, Spalletti initially denies everything. He tells poorly constructed stories, attempts to explain away the inconsistencies, and contradicts himself. After six hours of interrogation, he finally admits to being near the crime scene on the night of the murder and claims he returned home at midnight, just as his friend had done. But his wife contradicts him, stating clearly that she did not see him until around 2 am, when she herself was going to bed.

During the wife's interrogation, another critical piece of information emerges. She explains that Spalletti mentioned specific details about the double homicide before they were publicly known. At that point, detectives decide to arrest him. Spalletti insists he is innocent, but once he is behind bars he becomes silent. He refuses to elaborate. He offers no explanation for his earlier claims. His behavior grows more ambiguous.

In one of his rare statements, he tells investigators:

"You people know that I am not the killer, but you're keeping me imprisoned because you are protecting someone else."

His words add new layers of confusion to an already opaque situation. During Spalletti's imprisonment, an unknown caller contacts his wife and his brother. The message is cryptic and threatening:

"Tell him to be quiet and not to worry. He will soon be acquitted, he will soon be released from jail… but a little jail time will serve him well, that idiot. What was he thinking saying that he knew of the victims from the newspapers when the newspapers themselves didn't come out with the news until the following morning?"

The caller's identity is never discovered. Spalletti remains in jail until the Monster's next homicide. After his release, he never makes another public statement about the case. He does not collaborate with investigators, at least not in any official capacity. He is definitively acquitted in 1989.

Looking back with decades of hindsight and greater knowledge of the case's evolution, it becomes clear that the handling of the Spalletti matter was deeply flawed. Detectives were under intense pressure to produce results. The public was frightened. Newspapers demanded answers. In that environment, the decision to bring Spalletti in abruptly, based on minimal clues, may have been counterproductive. If they had chosen instead to follow him discreetly, observe his movements, and conduct a more thorough preliminary investigation, Spalletti might not have been frightened into silence. He might have served as a significant witness. Instead, he became another unsolved variable.

The Spalletti affair also exposed the existence of a widespread underground world of voyeurs, nocturnal wanderers who hid in fields and forests to spy on couples. For many citizens, the revelation of this secret community was shocking. Behind the well-polished public face of Florence, behind its esteemed cultural legacy and the image of a refined European city, lurked a darker behavioral ecosystem. Rumors even suggested that certain members of the city's elite engaged in similar nighttime activity.

This atmosphere of fear and moral panic made it unlikely that other "indians" would come forward. Many were married. Many held respectable jobs. None wanted to risk public humiliation. And so, whatever they may have heard or seen on that moonless night remained hidden.

Even today, many questions remain unanswered. What did Spalletti truly witness? Did he see the crime itself, or did he arrive moments after? Why did he initially speak about the murders, revealing details nobody could know? Why did he then fall into total silence? Was he threatened into submission? If so, by whom? And how many other voyeurs may have heard a sound, glimpsed a shadow, or noticed something unusual that night, and chose to bury the memory out of fear?

These questions hover like ghosts over the entire Monster of Florence investigation. They remind us how fragile truth becomes when fear, shame, and secrecy intertwine. The story of that night is not only about the Monster's cruelty. It is also about the voices that were silenced, willingly or not, and the clues that might have been lost forever in the dark fields surrounding the nightclub Anastasia.

Giovanni Foggi and
Carmela De Nuccio.

Italian daily newspaper of
the time.

The lifeless body of Carmela De Nuccio.

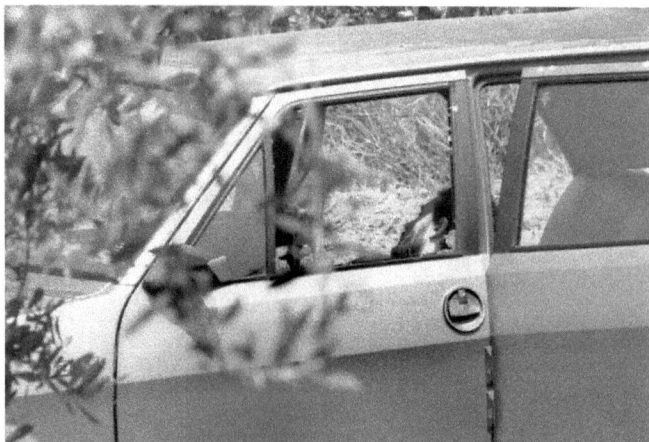

The lifeless body of Giovanni Foggi inside the car.

The blood drips inside Giovanni Foggi's car.

OCTOBER 22, 1981

Place: Le Bartoline, about 30 kilometers
from Florence.

It is a rather cold evening, the kind that marks the transition from the last breaths of summer into the steady arrival of fall. The Tuscan countryside feels different during this time of year. The air becomes sharper, the nights grow longer, and the fields around Florence begin to take on an austere, muted tone. On this particular night, Stefano Baldi and Susanna Cambi are driving through an obscure, isolated pathway that leads to an abandoned farmhouse. The area is remote, without streetlights, surrounded by patches of overgrown vegetation and long stretches of silence. For most people, the shadows in such a place would be unsettling. For couples looking for privacy, however, these hidden corners often offered the peace they sought.

Stefano is a twenty-six-year-old textile worker, known for his reliability and steady character. Susanna, twenty-four, works as an office employee. Their relationship is a serious one, built gradually over time, and the two have already begun planning to get married. Friends and relatives describe them as a grounded young couple, focused on building a future together. They had spent that night dining at Stefano's house, a simple, quiet evening that reflected the nature of their bond.

After dinner, at around 10 pm, they left in Stefano's black Volkswagen Golf, telling Stefano's parents that they were heading to the movies. Perhaps that had been their plan, or perhaps they simply wanted some time alone. By now, everyone in the area had heard about the June murders. The news had generated fear, speculation, and endless conversations. Yet as often happens, people convince themselves that tragedies strike elsewhere, always affecting others. Besides, the location of the June homicide felt far enough away. In the minds of Stefano and Susanna, there was likely no real danger.

What happens next takes place in the dark, with no witnesses to describe the sequence of events. Early the next morning, two retired locals walking through the area notice the black Golf abandoned in the pathway. At first, it seems like an ordinary case of a stalled car or a couple sleeping inside. As they approach, however, they are confronted with a scene of horror. Stefano and Susanna lie on the ground, both dead.

Stefano's body shows four gunshot wounds. At least two of the bullets are instantly fatal, hitting his heart. After being shot, he is stabbed four times post-mortem. The wounds display a fury that stands in contrast with the killer's habitual precision with firearms. Susanna's fate is equally brutal. According to the official reconstruction, she is shot five times, then pulled out of the passenger seat and dragged roughly ten meters away from the vehicle. There, her pubic area is mutilated, repeating the same ritualistic act seen in previous killings. In her hand she tightly clutches a chunk of hair. Investigators initially assume the hair may belong to Stefano. Yet this piece of evidence mysteriously disappears from the evidence room, adding another layer of doubt, confusion, and suspicion to the case.

Stefano, too, is dragged from the car. His body is placed on the ground near the driver's side. According to the official account, his body had been obstructing the killer's movement as he pulled Susanna out. For this reason, the killer supposedly dragged Stefano's corpse out of the way. Some investigators later suggest that the driver's side door may have been blocked, forcing the killer to extract Stefano's body through the passenger side. If that is the case, Stefano's body would then have been carried around the vehicle before being placed on the driver's side. The separation of the victims becomes a point of debate and analysis. Some experts interpret this movement as a strong, uncontrollable instinct on the part of the killer, perhaps revealing one of the only consistent psychological motives that ties all the murders together.

Years later, a new interpretation emerges, one based on a deeper analysis of details and on developments in the broader investigation. This interpretation suggests that Stefano and Susanna may have attempted to escape. According to this theory, they may have sensed something that alarmed them—perhaps a noise, a shadow, or a presence near the car. The possibility of two killers being present that night is also raised. However, the lack of visible dragging marks around the vehicle complicates any hypothesis. As in previous cases, the killer—or killers—ransacked the girl's purse. It is impossible to determine whether anything was taken from it.

At the crime scene, investigators find a shoe print, size 11, near the car. Not far from the vehicle, they also discover a black basalt stone shaped like a truncated pyramid. This strange object does not fit with the natural environment of the area. Its presence sparks curiosity among the detectives, though no definitive explanation is ever reached. Whether it fell, was dropped, or was carried to the scene remains a mystery.

During the early hours of the morning, before the bodies are officially discovered, an unsettling event takes place. A man tries to contact Susanna's mother by phone. He claims to have important news about her daughter. Yet almost immediately, the call is cut off due to a breakdown in the telephone system. The most disturbing part of this detail is that, in the days leading up to the murder, Susanna and her mother had been staying at the home of Susanna's aunt. Their temporary telephone number was not listed in any phone directory. Only people who knew them personally would have had access to that number, raising questions that remain unanswered.

At the time of the Baldi-Cambi double homicide, Enzo Spalletti is still in prison, accused of being the Monster. His arrest had been based on contradictions in his statements and on suspicious details about his presence near a previous crime scene. Yet this new murder clearly proves he cannot be the killer. As soon as the investigators confirm this, Spalletti is released and all charges against him are formally dropped. The authorities, under public pressure, now find themselves back at the starting point.

The Baldi-Cambi murders deepen the terror that has been growing in the region. Once again, the killer strikes with precision, cruelty, and a ritualistic signature. Once again, he leaves behind a scene designed to confuse, disturb, and challenge investigators. And once again, Tuscany awakens to a nightmare that leaves more questions than answers.

Stefano Baldi e Susanna Cambi.

Stefano Baldi's car at the crime scene.

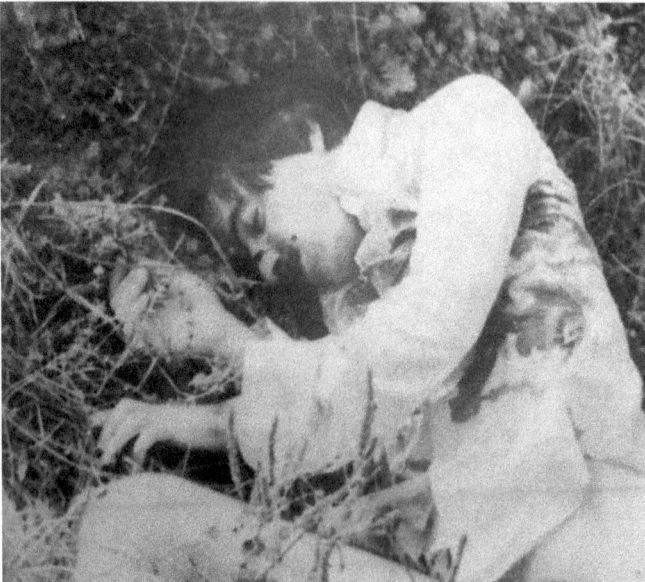
The body of Stefano Baldi.

The body of Susanna Cambi.

JUNE 19, 1982

Place: Baccaiano, 25 kilometers
from Florence.

It is around 11:15 PM when a friend of the
couple notices a Fiat 127 parked in a narrow
alleyway near the center of Baccaiano. This is not
a random sighting. The car belongs to Paolo
Mainardi, a twenty-four-year-old mechanic,
known in the village as a quiet, hardworking
young man. Paolo's girlfriend, nineteen-year-old
Antonella Migliorini, a tailor employed by a textile
company, is with him inside the vehicle. Their
relationship is strong and affectionate. Their
friends jokingly call them *Vinavil*, after the Italian
glue brand, to highlight how inseparable they are.
Wherever Paolo goes, Antonella is at his side, and

the same is true for her. They move together, think together, live within each other's rhythm.

Like every young person in the area, they have heard about the Monster. The stories circulate through bars, gas stations, workplaces, and family dinners. Fear mixes with disbelief. People reassure themselves by saying that such crimes only happen to others, that the victims were careless, that if one avoids dark, isolated places, one stays safe. Antonella in particular is known to be cautious. Her friends say she refuses to stop in isolated, hidden spots. She chooses visible, well-trafficked areas, precisely because she is frightened by what has been happening around Florence. But fear and caution are not enough. On that night, the Monster is nearby, and he has already chosen his target.

Between 11:40 PM and midnight, two friends drive past Paolo's car on their way to a bar in Baccaiano. They notice the Fiat 127 on the opposite side of the road. The car is at an odd angle. The front wheels are suspended in the air, while the rear wheels sit deep in a ditch. It looks like a trivial accident, something caused by a moment of distraction or a sudden maneuver. The friends continue toward the village only to find the bar closed. On their way back, they decide to stop and take a closer look at Paolo's car. The position of the vehicle raises suspicion.

The angle is strange. The setting is wrong. Something feels off.

As they approach the car, another couple arrives. This second couple was about five hundred meters away earlier in the night and had heard gunshots. They had seen strange movements in the darkness coming from the direction of the ditch. Unsettled and alarmed, they now approach the Fiat 127 with growing anxiety. What they see confirms their worst fears. A hole in the windshield, consistent with a bullet entry point. And behind the shattered glass, Paolo moves weakly, barely able to lift an arm. The scene is no accident. It is a shooting, and the attacker could still be nearby.

The two young men sprint toward the village to call the *carabinieri*, one of Italy's main police forces. The couple calls the ambulance. Time now becomes a race between rescue and the irreversible decline of two young lives. When the paramedics arrive, they struggle to extract the bodies from the vehicle. The driver's side door is jammed. The car's fall into the ditch has bent the metal frame enough to make it almost impossible to open the door without applying significant force. The passenger's side door is locked from the inside.

Paolo is eventually pulled out and rushed to the hospital, still alive but gravely wounded. He dies a few hours later without ever regaining consciousness. Antonella is declared dead at the scene. She is found on the back seat of the car when the *carabinieri* arrive. According to paramedics, Paolo's body was also in the back seat next to hers. But this conflicts with the testimony of the men who first discovered the scene, who insist Paolo was originally behind the wheel.

From the very beginning, this homicide becomes one of the most debated in the entire Monster of Florence investigation. Even the positions of the bodies raise contradictory interpretations. Theories develop, overlap, collapse, and evolve.

According to the official reconstruction, the killer either fired shaky, imprecise shots while the car was still parked in the alleyway, or the couple heard a noise and became alarmed. Paolo, frightened, engages the reverse gear and crosses the road in an attempt to escape. But perhaps due to nerves or panic, he loses control of the car. The rear wheels slip into the ditch. The vehicle becomes trapped, powerless. The Monster approaches. With two precise shots, he eliminates the headlights, extinguishing the bright beams that illuminate him and make both him and the scene visible to passersby. In the dark, he fires again, killing the couple.

Then, in a gesture both calculated and chilling, he reaches into the car, grabs the keys, locks the passenger's door—possibly to slow rescue efforts—and disappears into the night. It is a narrative that fits certain details but contradicts others.

The paramedics' testimony remains problematic. They insist Paolo was found in the back seat. Photographs taken at the scene show a streak of blood running down the driver's-side door in a perfect perpendicular line. If the car had already fallen into the ditch when that blood had been deposited, the streak should have slanted following the angle of the tilted car. Instead, the blood falls vertically, suggesting it was produced while the vehicle was still on level ground.

This discrepancy fuels alternative theories.

Some investigators claim the attack was swift and precise and occurred while the car was still in the pathway. According to this scenario, after shooting the couple, the Monster gets into the vehicle and puts it in reverse to move it away from the exposed area. His goal, perhaps, is to reach a more isolated spot to perform his ritualistic mutilations. But something goes wrong. He loses control—whether due to inexperience, panic, or the injured body of Paolo reacting unexpectedly—and the car plunges into the ditch.

Seeing the mistake, and aware that cars could pass at any moment on that road, he abandons the plan. He exits the vehicle, locks the door, removes the key, and flees.

Another interpretation suggests that Paolo fought back longer than assumed. Perhaps Paolo was still alive, behind the wheel, trying to start the car while Antonella remained in the back seat. The Monster then enters the car from the driver's side, shoots Paolo again or pushes him aside, dragging him toward the back seat and leaving the perpendicular streak of blood photographed on the door. He then attempts to reverse the car himself and loses control. This scenario reconciles more clues than the official reconstruction, but like all theories in the Monster of Florence case, it cannot be confirmed.

So what exactly happened that night? Every version raises questions the facts do not fully answer.

Where was the killer planning to go when he got behind the wheel of the car? Was he simply trying to move the vehicle a few meters, away from the main road, to perform his excision ritual? Or had he prepared an isolated spot in advance? Had he been watching the area earlier that evening, identifying possible escape routes?

Was this behavior unique to this homicide or part of an evolving modus operandi?

If we accept the official reconstruction, we face another question: Why did the Monster persist in an attack that was immediately complicated by Paolo's reaction? Why continue shooting, moving, and struggling around a car that was suddenly in the middle of the road, visible to anyone approaching? Why risk being seen by other drivers? Why not flee immediately?

One theory suggests that the killer behaved recklessly because he feared being recognized. According to this interpretation, Paolo or Antonella saw something—a detail of his face, his clothing, his vehicle—that could later identify him. If this were true, the Monster might have chosen to kill them at any cost rather than allow them to survive.

Paolo's final hours play a crucial role in the mythology of this case. At the hospital, he never regains consciousness. Yet Silvia Della Monica, the prosecutor, makes a strategic decision. She instructs journalists to publish that Paolo, before dying, provided important information for the investigation. This statement is false, but she hopes it will pressure the Monster, push him into a mistake, force him into a corner where he might reveal himself.

Not long after the article is printed, something disturbing happens. Lorenzo Alleganti, the ambulance driver who transported Paolo, receives a phone call. The caller has no noticeable accent and introduces himself as an investigator, asking what Paolo said before dying. Alleganti refuses to speak. The caller hangs up, then calls back seconds later. This time he identifies himself as the Monster. He threatens Alleganti, warning him not to repeat anything about the phone call.

The calls do not end there. According to Alleganti, similar calls continue until the end of 1985. One even reaches him at a boarding house in the Riviera Romagnola where he is vacationing. How the caller found the number remains unexplained.

Following this homicide, Marshal Francesco Fiori of the *carabinieri* recalls another murder from years earlier—fourteen years earlier, in the town of Signa. That case already had a culprit, someone who was behind bars in 1974 and therefore could not have committed the Monster's known crimes. Yet when investigators revisit the old case file, they find something shocking: brass .22 shells. Ballistics experts confirm they were fired by the same gun used in the Monster killings. This becomes the official narrative.

But some investigators and researchers doubt that story. They believe the link between the 1968 murder and the Monster case began only after anonymous letters reached the *carabinieri*. According to this alternate theory, the connection to Signa may have been a diversion orchestrated by the Monster, possibly with an accomplice tied to the Perugia tribunal, capable of inserting fabricated evidence into an old file. If true, the Monster might have intentionally redirected investigators down a path that would sabotage the entire investigation.

Supporters of this theory reject the idea that the 1968 homicide belongs to the Monster series. They believe the gun used in Signa was not the same as the one used in the later crimes. They argue that the attempt to link the cases was part of a strategy the Monster executed a few weeks after the Baccaiano homicide—precisely when anxiety about Paolo Mainardi possibly revealing something was at its peak.

This leads to unsettling questions:

Why would the Monster risk fabricating evidence?

Was he afraid Paolo had spoken before dying?

Did he fear that Paolo recognized him?

Did Paolo say something in the car, in the chaos of the attack, that threatened to expose him?

Did Antonella see more than the killer expected?

Was the Monster working alone, or was someone else involved that night?

The Baccaiano homicide does not provide answers. It opens doors, multiplies theories, deepens contradictions. More than any other attack, this one shows the Monster's unpredictability, his willingness to improvise, his growing recklessness, and perhaps his growing fear.

This is why the killing of Paolo Mainardi and Antonella Migliorini remains one of the most debated chapters in the entire Monster of Florence case—a night where the darkness is not enough to hide the truth, and the truth remains forever trapped inside a Fiat 127 stranded in a ditch on a quiet Tuscan road.

Antonella Migliorini and Paolo Mainardi.

The lifeless body of Antonella Migliorini inside the car.

The bullet hole in Paolo's car windshield.

Baccaiano, crime scene.

Baccaiano, crime scene.

Paolo Mainardi's car.

Paolo Mainardi's car.

Baccaiano, crime scene.

The lifeless body of Antonella Migliorini inside the car.

Baccaiano, crime scene.

AUGUST 21, 1968

Place: Signa, about 20 kilometers
from Florence.

It is about 2 AM on August 21, 1968, when
Mr. De Felice is startled awake by the sound of
his doorbell ringing insistently. At that hour, in
the stillness of a summer night, any noise feels
amplified, but a doorbell at 2 AM is alarming in
itself. Confused and uneasy, he steps out onto his
balcony to see who could possibly be calling at
such an hour. What he sees below is a scene that
will stay with him for the rest of his life,
something that feels more like the opening of a
horror film than real life.

Standing alone in the darkness, barefoot, pale,
and trembling, is a child. A boy no older than six.
His hair is messy, his eyes wide not with panic but

with the numb exhaustion of someone who has endured something far beyond his understanding. When he tilts his face upward toward De Felice, his voice is small and strangely calm. He simply says:

«Open the door because I am sleepy and daddy is in bed, sick. After, you take me home because mommy and my uncle are dead in the car.»

The words fall heavy in the night. They make no sense at first, and yet the boy states them with such clarity that De Felice feels an immediate chill run down his spine. Something terrible has happened. Something far beyond what a child should ever witness. Without wasting a moment, he calls the *carabinieri*.

When the officers arrive, they follow the boy's quiet, precise indications. He walks ahead of them, barefoot on gravel, guiding them to a car parked near the cemetery of Signa. And inside the vehicle, exactly as he said, they find the bodies of the boy's mother and her lover. The scene is grim. Barbara Locci, a thirty-two-year-old housewife, and Antonio Lo Bianco, a twenty-nine-year-old laborer, lie dead together.

According to the official reconstruction, the two lovers had spent the evening at the movies. Afterward, seeking privacy, they had driven to the quiet area near the cemetery. But they had not been alone. With them was Barbara's son, little Natalino, who was inside the car when the attack occurred and who miraculously survived.

Barbara was married to Stefano Mele, Natalino's father. The couple, like many Sardinians of that era, had moved to the Florentine area in search of work and a better future. Their marriage, however, was complicated. Barbara had numerous lovers—something that was widely known. Interestingly, Mele seemed to accept her affairs with unusual resignation. He never appeared jealous, nor did he take any visible action to stop them. For this reason, when the *carabinieri* immediately target him as the prime suspect, the case already contains an element of contradiction.

Still, jealousy is an easy narrative, and in the initial hours investigators cling to the simplest hypothesis: a husband discovers his wife's betrayal, snaps, and kills her and her lover in a violent rage. Mele is brought in for questioning. At first, he denies everything. Then, under pressure, he begins accusing others—other Sardinians, acquaintances, even some of Barbara's former lovers. Eventually, after a series of contradictory statements, he confesses.

His confession, however, is frail and unconvincing. The weapon used in the murder is never found. Mele claims he threw it into a ditch, but he is unable to describe exactly where or how. Despite the gaps, he is sentenced. The case is declared closed. The tragedy of 1968 is filed away, considered solved.

For more than a decade, nothing changes. Life moves on. The story fades into memory, except for those who lived it. But Mele's conviction, flimsy as it was, stands—until the early 1980s.

By the end of 1982, Tuscany is shaken by a series of double homicides later attributed to the Monster of Florence. The pattern, the weapon, the brutality: everything pushes investigators into a corner. They search for connections, hidden links, traces of the killer's past. And it is during this period that the 1968 case resurfaces.

Marshal Francesco Fiori, relying on what he calls a sudden flash of memory—or perhaps influenced by the anonymous letters that begin arriving at the *carabinieri* barracks—suggests reexamining the old Signa case. When investigators reopen the file, they begin noticing similarities: the type of victims, the positioning of the bodies, the type of gun used. The connection appears possible. Even disturbing.

Attention quickly shifts to a man who had hovered on the margins of the 1968 investigation: Francesco Vinci. A Sardinian immigrant like Mele, Vinci has a long criminal past, a history marked by violence, and a reputation that makes him an easy target for suspicion. He had once been Barbara Locci's lover, and his involvement in the 1968 case had been mentioned—then withdrawn—during Mele's unstable confession.

Now, with the Monster of Florence case exploding in complexity, Vinci suddenly looks like a potential key. His record is troubling. He has been accused multiple times of domestic violence against his wife. His personality is described as rough, impulsive, often aggressive. To the eyes of investigators desperate for leads, Vinci has all the right—or wrong—ingredients. He seems capable of violence. He has an emotional link to the earlier crime. And crucially, his presence in the vicinity of several Monster crime scenes can be confirmed for the periods in which the murders occurred.

For a moment, it seems like the puzzle is coming together. The Monster must be Vinci.

But before investigators can push further in this direction, something happens—something that was feared and yet, in some hidden way, expected. While Vinci is still in prison, held under the suspicion of being the Monster, the real killer strikes again.

This single act changes everything.

It destroys the hypothesis built around Vinci. It undermines the assumptions of the investigators. It reopens the 1968 case entirely. And it forces everyone to confront the uncomfortable truth that the killer is still out there, still hunting, still observing, still choosing his victims with terrifying precision.

From that moment on, the story begins to twist. Evidence is reinterpreted, theories are rewritten, alliances shift among investigators, and the long chain linking 1968 to the later murders becomes the source of endless conflict.

What seemed like a closed case suddenly becomes the first chapter in a nightmare that will haunt Tuscany for decades.

Barbara Locci and Antonio Lo Bianco.

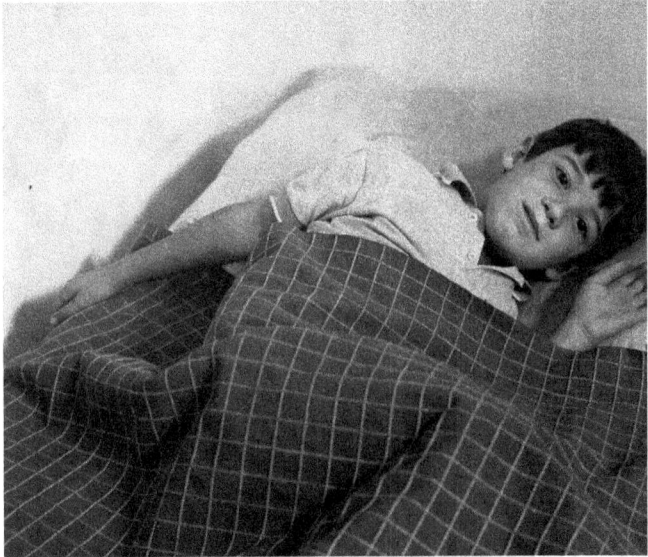

Natalino Mele.

Signa, crime scene.

Stefano Mele at the crime scene with the *Carabinieri*.

Antono Lo Bianco's car.

Signa, crime scene.

SEPTEMBER 9, 1983

Place: Giogoli, about 10 kilometers from Florence.

The scene that appears before the eyes of Rolf Reinecke, the first person to discover the double homicide, is surreal to the point of disorientation. It is early morning, the hour uncertain, the light still dim. Reinecke, who resides at the nearby villa "La Sfacciata," is accustomed to the quiet rhythms of the countryside outside Florence. Nothing in his daily life prepares him for what he is about to witness as he approaches the unusual sight of a parked Volkswagen van.

At first, the vehicle seems out of place. It is one of those iconic vans made popular by the American TV series *On the Road*, painted in faded colors and equipped for travel. Its presence near the villa might have passed as simple tourism, something common in Tuscany in the early 1980s. But the details surrounding the van quickly shatter any sense of normalcy. The plates are German. The sliding door is slightly ajar. And from inside, echoing into the morning silence, the soundtrack of *Blade Runner* plays on infinite autoreverse, looping over and over in a mechanical, almost hypnotic repetition.

The music, synthetic and melancholic, fills the air with a science-fiction eeriness. It becomes the soundtrack not of a film, but of a crime scene.

Reinecke steps closer. Winchester bullet shells —caliber .22, H series—are scattered on the ground near the van. Their metallic glint contrasts with the dusty earth. Later, loose pages from a homosexual pornographic magazine will be found nearby, fluttering slightly in the breeze, as if someone had tossed them carelessly or placed them there intentionally.

Inside the van lie the victims: two twenty-four-year-old German students from the University of Münster, both on a summer vacation in Italy. Their names are Horst Meyer and Uwe Rüsch. They had been traveling together, exploring Tuscany in their van, reading, listening to music, and enjoying the freedom of the road. They were likely doing exactly that when the Monster attacked.

According to forensic reconstruction, the Monster shot the young men while they were inside the van, possibly relaxed and unaware of the danger. The first shots are fired from outside, through the right side window. Experts conclude that the initial two bullets were fired from a distance of about forty centimeters from the glass. Then, the killer allegedly moved to the left side of the vehicle and fired three more shots from that position. Afterward, he is believed to have entered the van, firing two additional shots from inside.

The precision of the shots is once again unmistakable. The Monster's marksmanship is evident, consistent with previous murders. The angles of the bullet holes in the van's body allow investigators to estimate the shooter's height at approximately 1.80 meters or possibly even taller. But this conclusion is immediately met with skepticism from some investigators, who argue that the shooter's height could vary significantly based on his posture, the angle of his arms, and the position of the gun. A crouched stance, a raised arm, or the use of the van's structure as support could distort measurements. As with everything in the Monster case, certainty is elusive.

Following this crime, investigators find themselves once again plunged into confusion. The Monster has altered the pattern. Until now, all of the known victims were heterosexual couples—young men and women attacked while seeking privacy. But these victims are two men. Two foreign men. And their sexual orientation remains unclear.

Did the Monster make a mistake?

Did he fire without realizing that one of the silhouettes belonged to a male and not a female? Or—and this possibility is far more troubling—did he deliberately choose a couple of two men?

Speculation spreads quickly among investigators and later among journalists and the public. Some detectives wonder whether the Monster had been unable to find an Italian couple that night and targeted the Germans instead. Others consider that he may have followed these two young men on purpose, perhaps after observing them somewhere earlier in the evening.

The pornographic magazine found near the van raises even more questions. It is titled *Golden Gay*, a homosexual publication. To some investigators, its presence is suspicious. The magazine is in excellent condition despite being outdoors, and no fingerprints are found on it. According to those who believe the Monster staged parts of his crime scenes, this detail suggests that he brought the magazine with him. If true, the implication becomes chilling: the Monster may have planned to kill two men that night, choosing them according to a script he crafted for reasons unknown, and planting the magazine to push the investigation in a certain direction—or simply to mock investigators.

While these debates unfold, one thing becomes clear: the main suspect of recent months, Francesco Vinci, could not be the killer. Vinci, the violent Sardinian with a criminal history, the man who had been portrayed by the press and much of public opinion as the face of the Monster, is in prison when the homicide occurs. His alibi is absolute. This crime clears him completely. But ironically, it is this exoneration that puts him in danger.

A few years later, Vinci is found dead. His burned body, bound and charred, is discovered inside his car along with another Sardinian man, Angelo Vargiu. The murder is brutal and symbolic. Some believe it is linked to the Monster case, perhaps revenge or an attempt to silence someone who knew too much. But others, particularly those familiar with Sardinian criminal networks, assert that the killing has nothing to do with the Monster. To them, it looks like a mafia-style execution, a payback related to disputes within Sardinian criminal groups living in Tuscany.

With Vinci now definitively eliminated as a suspect, the investigators shift their attention once again to the group of Sardinians connected to the 1968 Locci-Lo Bianco homicide—the one involving Barbara Locci, her lover Antonio Lo Bianco, and the little boy Natalino. This circle includes several of the same names that have repeatedly surfaced: Stefano Mele, the convicted husband; Giovanni Mele, his brother; and Piero Mucciarini, his brother-in-law.

Stefano Mele's shifting, contradictory statements had, at one point or another, implicated almost every Sardinian man he knew. For years, these declarations had been dismissed as unreliable, confused, or the ramblings of a jealous husband under pressure. But now, with fresh doubt cast over earlier assumptions, investigators revisit those testimonies.

Based on fragments of clues, partial accusations, and a growing need to isolate suspects, Giovanni Mele and Piero Mucciarini are arrested and imprisoned. They remain behind bars, becoming the new "Sardinian suspects" in the eyes of the public and the press.

But just as before—just as when Francesco Vinci was imprisoned—the Monster strikes again.

And once again, everything collapses.

The pattern repeats:

A suspect is arrested.

Investigators feel they are close to a breakthrough.

Public pressure eases for a moment.
And then the Monster kills again, proving definitively that the wrong man is behind bars.

This cycle of false certainty and violent correction becomes one of the defining elements of the entire Monster of Florence saga. It highlights the fragility of the investigation, the lack of a coherent strategy, and the desperation of authorities who, under immense public scrutiny, continue to chase shadows rather than the killer himself.

After the murder of the two German students, the Monster's crimes no longer seem tied exclusively to romantic couples or to the narrative of sexual jealousy that has fueled earlier interpretations. Instead, the killer appears increasingly unpredictable, perhaps experimenting with new patterns, perhaps sending a message, or perhaps acting according to a logic known only to himself.

For the investigators, this double homicide marks yet another descent into darkness, another dead end, and another reminder that the Monster remains several steps ahead—hidden, calculating, uncatchable.

And Tuscany, once again, wakes up to fear.

Horst Wilhelm Meyer and Jens-Uwe Rüsch.

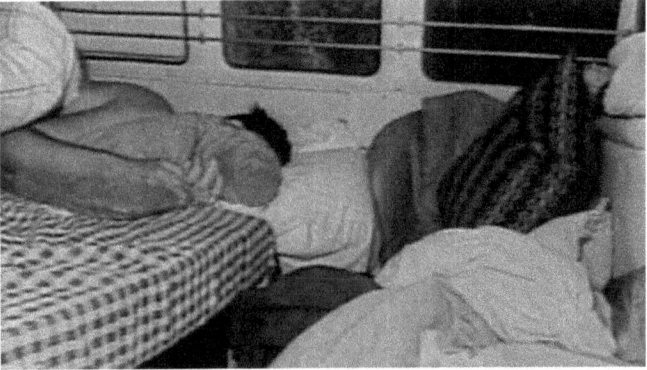

The lifeless bodies of the two German teenagers
inside the Volkswagen van.

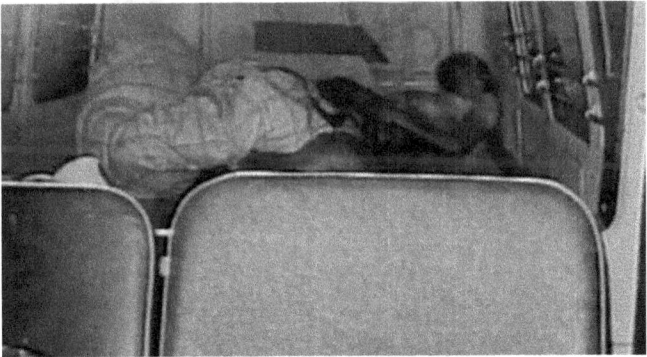

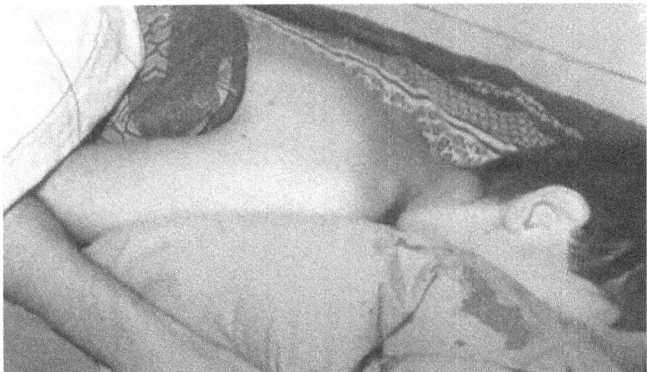

Giogoli, crime scene.

Giogoli, crime scene.

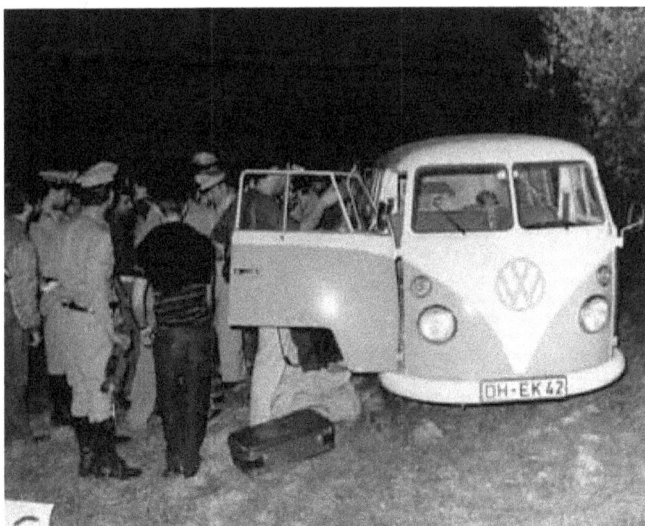

JULY 29, 1984

Place: Boschetta di Vicchio, about 30
kilometers from Florence.

Pia Rontini had only recently entered
adulthood. At eighteen, she was full of the quiet
hopes and early ambitions typical of someone
beginning to step into their own life. She had just
started a new job as a bartender in a bar not far
from home, a position she appreciated because it
allowed her to meet people, feel independent, and
begin contributing to her own future while
staying close to her family. Her mother, proud of
her daughter's initiative, often waited for her at
home to share small moments of daily life. On
the evening in question, however, an unexpected
shift change meant that Pia returned home earlier
than usual. Instead of working late, she found

herself sitting at the dinner table with her mother, sharing a meal that would tragically become their last together.

It is around 9 PM when Pia, following her mother's suggestion, decides to go out and meet her boyfriend, Claudio Stefanacci. Claudio is twenty-one years old, a student with a calm and caring temperament. Friends describe the couple as young but solid, affectionate, and sincerely devoted to one another. Pia and Claudio had made plans to spend some time together that night, probably just driving around, talking, and enjoying the cool summer air. Claudio picks her up, and the two drive off in his FIAT Panda, intending to spend a peaceful evening. Nothing suggests danger, nothing indicates that their night will turn into one of the darkest moments in the long series of murders committed by the Monster.

Around 9:45 PM, a hunter walking in a wooded area with his wife hears five distinct shots. The sound is sharp, unnatural in the quiet countryside. He pauses, instinctively trying to determine the direction of the gunfire. But the night around him remains still. He assumes the shots may come from poachers or someone target-shooting illegally. With no further sounds, no cries for help, and nothing else to indicate danger, he continues his walk.

Hours later, however, those sounds will gain a chilling significance.

Around 3 AM, after a long and increasingly desperate search by the victims' families and local residents, the FIAT Panda is finally found in a small locality known as Boschetta, only a few minutes away from Claudio's home. The car is difficult to see in the dark. The area is poorly lit, surrounded by fields used for cultivating medicinal herbs, a type of crop that grows tall and thick. At night, the visibility here is extremely low.

The vehicle looks immediately disturbed. The passenger-side window is shattered, and the two front seats have been overturned as if a violent struggle or sudden intrusion occurred. The atmosphere around the car is heavy, quiet, almost unnaturally still—as though the countryside itself is holding its breath.

Claudio's body is discovered inside the vehicle, sprawled in the back seat. A careful examination reveals that he was hit by three gunshots. These wounds alone might not have immediately killed him, which means he likely remained conscious for a short period of time. The realization of this adds another layer of horror, since the autopsy later records ten stab wounds inflicted on his body. The blows are violent, delivered with frenzy and intensity, a signature element already familiar from previous Monster crimes. The pattern of violence suggests hatred, ritual, or a compulsion that goes far beyond a simple intent to kill.

Pia's body is found outside the car, a few meters away, lying on a narrow sidetrack. She was shot while still inside the vehicle—expertly, precisely. The bullets that strike her appear to have rendered her unconscious almost immediately. She likely never saw the killer up close, never had a chance to react. Her body shows signs of mutilation: her pubis has been removed, and so has her left breast. These post-mortem excisions replicate the ritualistic actions observed in earlier murders, indicating a repeated behavioral pattern.

On the right door of the car, investigators find an imprint believed to be left by the killer's knee as he leaned inside to shoot. Anthropometric tests performed on this impression confirm a height estimate of around 180 centimeters—consistent with the estimate obtained after examining evidence from the double homicide of the German victims. This consistency reinforces the hypothesis of a single perpetrator with a stable physical profile.

Despite the careful search conducted by investigators and forensic teams, no traces of the killer's escape are found. Not even footprints in the soft terrain, disturbed vegetation, or broken stems in the medicinal herb field surrounding the area. Under normal conditions, the micro-terrain around the Panda should have revealed at least minor signs—indentations, smudges, some element showing the path taken by whoever left the scene. Instead, the perimeter is clean, undisturbed.

Such an absence of trace suggests something significant: the Monster had likely scouted the location in advance, studying possible escape routes, identifying blind spots, and planning how to approach and leave the crime scene without leaving evidence. This careful preparation is consistent with earlier murders. The Monster appears not to strike impulsively but with a strategy shaped by reconnaissance, familiarity with the terrain, and a clinical level of caution.

There is another detail that becomes relevant. In the weeks before the murder, Pia confided to a Danish friend that she had encountered someone unsettling at the bar where she worked. She described a man who made her uncomfortable, someone who watched her too closely, someone who seemed to be following her. She told her friend she did not feel safe. Unfortunately, she did not know the man's name.

Another witness emerges later: the manager of a restaurant in San Piero a Sieve. He recalls having seen Pia and Claudio together at his establishment earlier that afternoon. They appeared relaxed, a normal couple. But the manager also remembers another individual in the restaurant—a "distinguished gentleman," as he described him. The man had red hair, wore a jacket and tie, and ordered a beer. What troubled the manager was the way this man behaved. He sat near the couple. He did not seem interested in his drink. Instead, he watched them attentively, almost studying them. When Pia and Claudio left the restaurant, the red-haired man got up and followed them outside.

This testimony sounds compelling, even eerie, but it comes with a complication. It contradicts other reconstructions of the victims' movements that day. Moreover, despite the unsettling nature of the description, the lead never produces concrete progress. The man is never identified. No matching suspect emerges. The testimony remains one more fragment—troubling, suggestive, but ultimately inconclusive.

The murders of Pia Rontini and Claudio Stefanacci deepen the terror in the region. The brutality inflicted on both victims, the precision of the shots, the absence of escape traces, and the suggestion of prior stalking point once again to a killer who prepares meticulously but acts with explosive, ritualistic violence. The Monster remains a ghost: seen by no one, leaving nothing behind, yet moving through the Tuscan night with purpose.

As with all the Monster's crimes, this case becomes another labyrinth of clues, contradictions, dead ends, and haunting possibilities—another chapter in a nightmare that continues to grow darker.

Pia Rontini and Claudio Stefanacci.

The reconstruction of the killer's height according to the forensic experts.

Claudio Stefanacci's car.

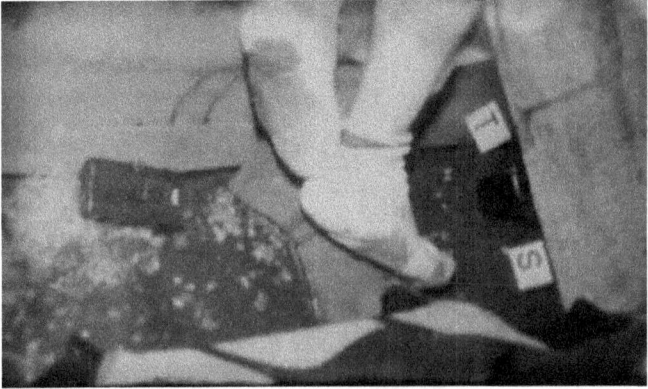

The interior of Claudio Stefanacci's car. The feet of
the poor victim are visible, with blood-stained socks

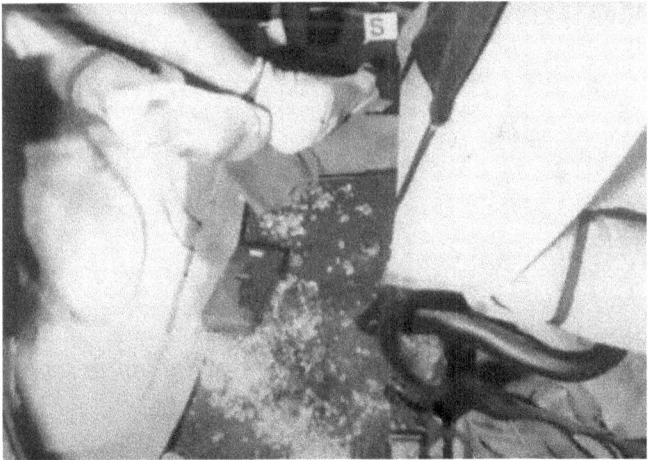

The lifeless body of Pia Rontini covered with a
sheet.

Law enforcement removing Pia Rontini's body from
the crime scene.

Some journalists, including Mario Spezi, at the crime scene in front of the lifeless body of poor Pia Rontini.

Claudio Stefanacci's car.

Front page of a newspaper from the time reporting the double murder in Vicchio.

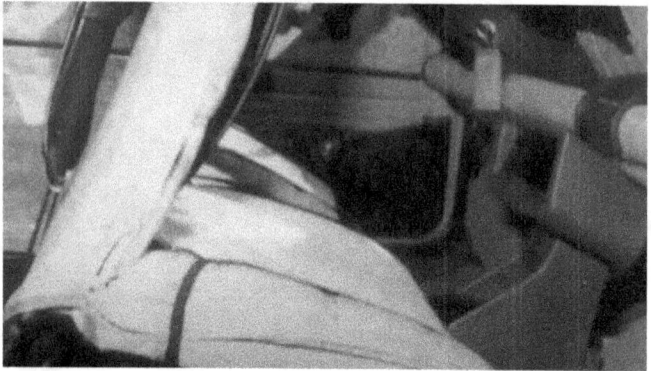

Claudio Stefanacci's car.

Front page of a newspaper from the time reporting the double murder in Vicchio.

The lifeless body of Pia Rontini covered with a sheet.

SEPTEMBER 7 OR 8, 1985
(DATE UNCERTAIN)

Place: Scopeti, 20 kilometers from Florence.

Jean Michel Kraveichvili and Nadine Mauriot had been traveling through Italy, enjoying the freedom of the open road and the warmth of late summer in Tuscany. They were young, in love, and eager to experience the quiet beauty of the countryside. Their trip had brought them to a clearing in San Casciano Val di Pesa, in the locality known as Scopeti, a place surrounded by woods and narrow dirt paths. They set up their Canadian tent in a small open space, away from large campgrounds and noise. For them, the isolation must have felt romantic, intimate, the ideal spot to spend the night under a soft September sky.

The approximate date of the homicide is placed between the night of September 8 and 9, although some experts consider the possibility that the murders occurred the night before, between September 7 and 8. This alternate estimate is based on the developmental stage of fly larvae found on Nadine's body, a detail that introduces uncertainty but also reflects the forensic challenges of a crime scene in the open countryside.

It is nighttime. The French couple is inside their tent, making love, immersed in darkness and surrounded by the stillness typical of rural Tuscany at that hour. The only sounds are those of insects, leaves shifting in the faint breeze, and perhaps the distant hum of a road. They are vulnerable, unaware that someone is approaching through the shadows.

According to one reconstruction accepted by many investigators, the killer approaches the tent quietly from the side facing the camping area. Using a blade, he slices through the outer fabric of the tent. It is an intentional, silent gesture— one that allows him to discern movement inside without alerting the couple. Then, he moves to the opposite side, positioning himself for the attack.

From there, he fires his weapon.

Shots rip through the tent's cloth. Nadine, who is likely on top of Jean Michel at that moment, is struck by several bullets. The wounds are instantly fatal. Jean Michel, though hit, is only superficially wounded. Realizing the danger, completely nude and fueled by adrenaline, he manages to reach the exit of the tent. He escapes into the dark woods, attempting to flee. Perhaps he thinks he can find help. Perhaps he hopes the attacker will chase only him, allowing Nadine a chance to survive. Or perhaps, in that moment of terror, he simply runs because instinct demands it.

But darkness offers no salvation.

The Monster catches up with him after only a few meters. Jean Michel tries to resist, but he is overpowered. The killer finishes him off with a knife. His body is later found partly concealed under debris—broken branches, pieces of junk abandoned in the clearing. It appears as though the Monster made a brief, half-hearted attempt to hide the body, though not enough to prevent its discovery.

Once Jean Michel is dead, the Monster returns to the tent. There, he performs the ritualistic mutilations that have become his signature. Evidence suggests that he remained inside the tent while carrying out part of the excision, as blood patterns and spatial traces indicate work done in the confined space. However, some investigators believe that he may have dragged Nadine's body outside at some point to gain freedom of movement or to better manage the positioning of the body before returning it inside. Whether this was an attempt to delay discovery or a matter of practicality remains unknown.

Nadine's pubis and left breast are removed, repeating the same pattern observed in previous murders. This reinforces the conclusion that the killing was part of the same series and that the perpetrator maintained a consistent ritual.

On Monday, September 9, in the early afternoon, the bodies are discovered by chance. A man searching for mushrooms in the woods catches a glimpse of something pale through the branches. He approaches and realizes he is looking at a human body. Terrified, he contacts the authorities. The *carabinieri* arrive on the scene and soon locate the tent, where they find Nadine's body. The identities of the victims are confirmed shortly thereafter. It is another double homicide. Another foreign couple. Another crime carried out with precision and ritualistic violence.

But the story does not end in the clearing.

On Tuesday, September 10—less than twenty-four hours after the discovery—a letter arrives at the prosecutor's office in Florence. It is addressed to "Dott Della Monica Silvia Public Prosecutor's Office." The address is immediately strange. Silvia Della Monica is no longer in charge of the Monster investigations; she had been replaced the previous year. The clerks, unaware of the envelope's significance, open it.

Inside is a strip of Nadine Mauriot's breast.

The envelope's exterior is even stranger. The address is composed of letters cut out from illustrated magazines, arranged like a ransom note. Experts later determine that the letters were cut with a blade, not scissors. This detail adds to the sense of calculation: the Monster seemed to want to avoid leaving the type of serrated or pressure marks that scissors produce. There also a spelling error: the word "Repubblica" is written with a single *b*.

To some investigators, this is a sign of poor education, suggesting a killer with limited schooling. Others, however, argue the opposite—that the mistake is deliberate. They believe it is a strategic diversion, designed to mislead investigators into assuming a social and cultural background lower than the killer's true one. These differing interpretations reflect the broader difficulty of the entire investigation: every piece of evidence can suggest multiple truths.

Forensic analysis determines that the letter was mailed no later than Monday morning. This means the Monster had collected the body part, prepared the package, and traveled to a post office early on September 9. The postmark confirms that the envelope was mailed from San Piero a Sieve, approximately sixty kilometers from Scopeti—far enough to complicate tracing but close enough to remain within the geography already associated with the Monster's prior movements.

No fingerprints are found on the envelope. No biological traces, no hair, no fibers. As always, the Monster leaves nothing behind. The letter is both a message and a challenge. It proves he is ahead of the investigators. It shows he is unafraid. And it deepens the psychological complexity of his crimes.

From that day forward, the Monster disappears once again. The killing stops. The mutilations stop. The letters stop. For years, nothing happens.

Silence takes the place of violence.

But the fear remains, lingering like a shadow across the Tuscan countryside. The Scopeti murders and the letter sent to the prosecutor's office become the final confirmed chapter in the Monster's long series of murders—a final act of brutality followed by a vanishing that leaves investigators with unanswered questions, conflicting theories, and a trail of evidence that will fuel decades of debate.

And Tuscany is left with the memory of a tent in a clearing, two young lives stolen, and a killer who once again slips into the night without leaving a trace.

Jean Michel Kraveichvili and Nadine Mauriot.

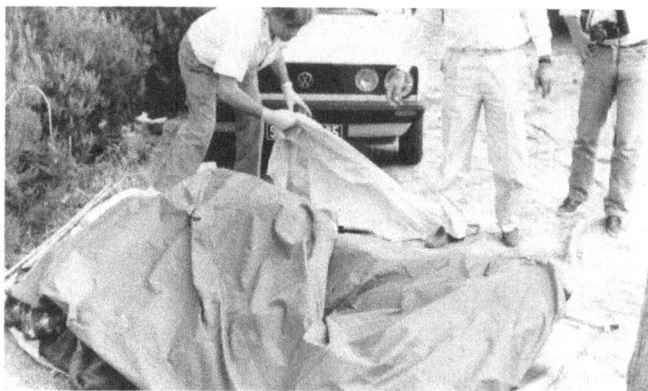

Scopeti, crime scene.

Scopeti, crime scene.

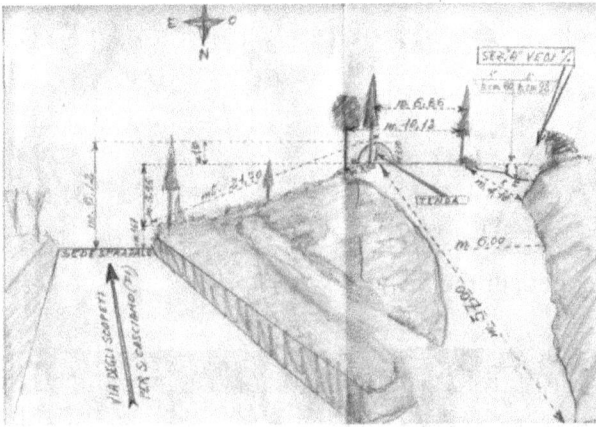

The official law enforcement reconstruction of the dynamics of the Scopeti double murder

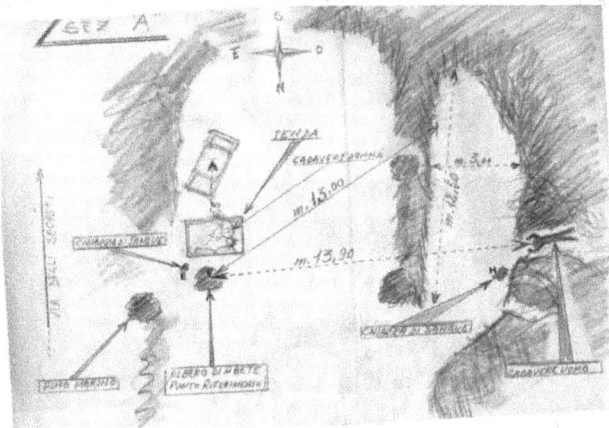

Scopeti, crime scene.

Journalists, *carabinieri*, and onlookers crowd the Scopeti crime scene. As you can clearly see in this period photo, and in others published on the previous pages, the Monster of Florence crime scenes were never secured, which led to irreversible contamination.

French newspapers also covered the case extensively.

Scopeti, crime scene.

Scopeti, crime scene.

Scopeti, crime scene.

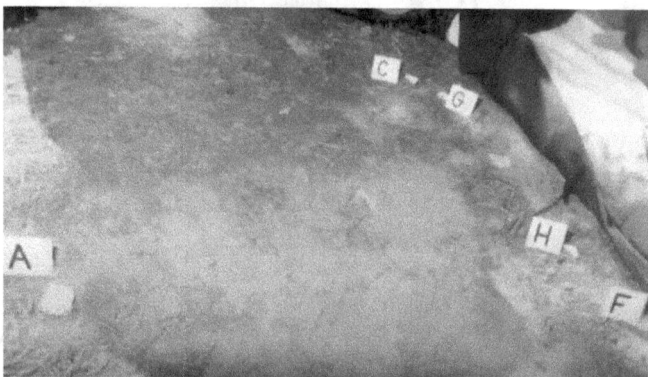

Scopeti, crime scene.

Scopeti, crime scene.

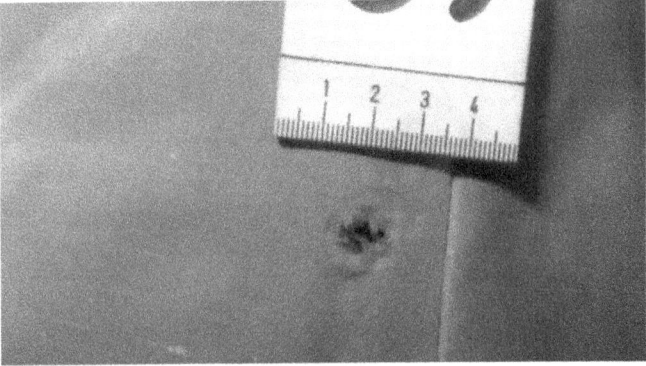

Photo of the bullet on the French couple's tent.

Scopeti, crime scene.

THE INVESTIGATIONS

The investigations into the crimes attributed to the Monster of Florence span a period of forty years, if we consider the 1968 double homicide as the starting point. Over these four decades, an extraordinary number of investigators, magistrates, forensic experts, and police officials have attempted to untangle this complex and elusive case. Hundreds of suspects, witnesses, informants, and peripheral figures have passed through interrogation rooms and court hearings for reasons ranging from direct involvement to mere coincidence.

Given this vast time frame and the enormous cast of individuals connected in one way or another to the case, it is easy to understand why investigative theories have remained so diverse.

Each investigator brought their own perspective, methods, and assumptions. As a result, even today, the case appears different depending on the angle from which it is examined. Some see a lone, meticulous serial killer. Others envision a network or group. Still others believe key evidence was misunderstood or deliberately manipulated.

What follows is a brief overview of the main investigative theories formulated over the years. Some were pursued for a period of time before being discarded, only to be revisited later with new details or renewed intuition. Others now appear outdated, products of their era. Each, however, contributes to the long and complicated history of one of Italy's most mysterious criminal investigations.

CLASSICAL
INVESTIGATIVE THEORY

The investigations into the 1968 crime focused immediately on the victim's family and closest relationships. Investigators examined every aspect of Barbara Locci's past, including her numerous romantic connections, friendships, and movements in the months before the murder. Very early on, the authorities believed that the figure of the assassin had to be found within the small circle of men surrounding her. The investigation followed a classic approach: identify a motive, link it to a suspect, and connect that suspect directly to the victim. Despite the controversy that later emerged, many people still argue that, for that specific homicide, investigators initially moved in a reasonable and logical direction.

The 1974 crime, however, was not connected to the 1968 murder. The six–year gap between the two events, combined with differences in the modality of the killing, discouraged any attempt to link them. Once again, investigators turned their attention to the lives of the victims, examining their routines, social relationships, and private affairs in the hope of identifying motives or personal conflicts capable of provoking such violence.

But very quickly, the clues collected after the 1974 crime began to collapse under scrutiny. Contradictions emerged, connections dissolved, and no clear personal motive could be established. As a result, the homicide was eventually attributed to a generic sexual maniac, a label used when no other explanation seemed to fit.

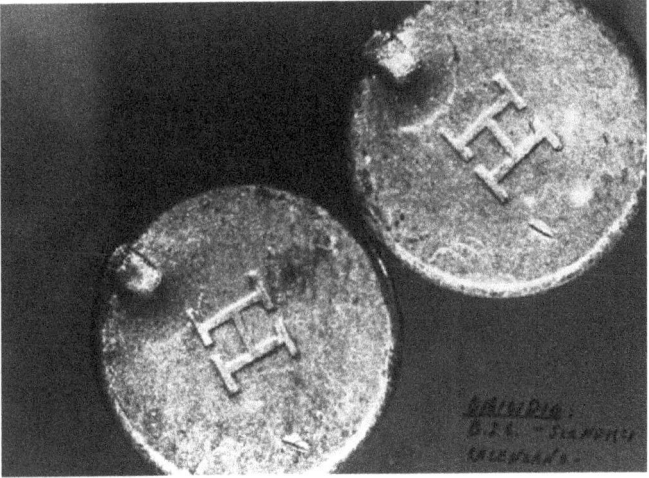

The Winchester .22 H-series shell casings used by the killer, showing the unmistakable "mark" left by the gun used by the Monster of Florence.

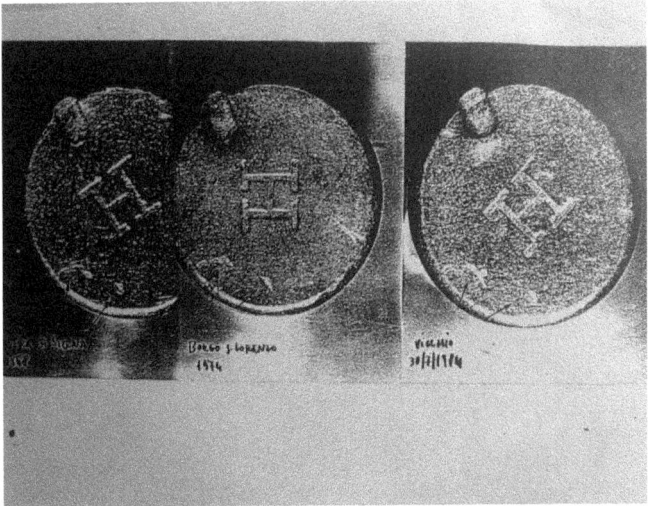

THE UNIQUE SERIAL KILLER
AND THE WORRISOME
COINCIDENCES

Let's start by saying that the very idea of a "serial killer," as we understand it today, was almost unknown in Italy during the early years of the Monster of Florence investigation. When the homicides began to accumulate and it was eventually established that the same weapon and the same modus operandi had been used, both the police and the press suddenly found themselves confronting a phenomenon for which they had neither cultural nor investigative preparation. Italy, up to that point, had known crimes of passion, mafia executions, political terrorism, kidnappings—but not a structured, ritualistic killer acting over many years. The term itself was foreign, and the mental framework needed to understand such a criminal simply was not part of Italian investigative training.

Faced with a new type of criminal, the classical tools of investigation quickly proved inadequate. Understanding the victims' social connections, friendships, and personal conflicts—an approach that works well with crimes driven by jealousy, revenge, or financial motives—offered little help. In these murders, the victims left behind no direct enemies, no obvious conflicts, no clear reasons that could explain such brutality. As the certainty grew that the killings were connected, the authorities entered a prolonged phase of uncertainty in which dozens of hypotheses were generated, discarded, revived, and reshaped over time.

One of the earliest lines of speculation focused on the killer's evident mastery in the use of knives and blades. He performed excisions with disturbing precision, suggesting familiarity with anatomy and cutting techniques. Some investigators theorized that the Monster might be a doctor or a surgeon, someone accustomed to handling scalpels and performing delicate incisions. Others countered that expertise with blades could also belong to a shoemaker, a butcher, or a skilled artisan—professions common in Tuscany. Studies on serial killers around the world later confirmed that many offenders are indeed "handy" people, individuals who work with their hands, who are confident with tools, and who feel at ease when performing practical tasks requiring coordination and calm.

Another widespread belief was geographical. The Monster clearly knew the Tuscan countryside. He understood the back roads, the provincial lanes, the isolated farm paths, and the quiet wooded areas where couples might stop. The ease with which he navigated these spaces indicated that he lived in the area, or at least spent significant time there. More specifically, because all the murders took place between late spring and early autumn, many investigators suggested that the Monster might live in the region during the summer—perhaps for seasonal work, or perhaps because he spent his vacations there. Others proposed that the timing reflected the behavioral patterns of the victims rather than those of the killer: couples were more likely to seek privacy outdoors on warm nights.

Another central question emerged: did the Monster choose his victims or did he choose the locations? Two opposing schools of thought developed. One theory proposed that the Monster followed specific couples for some time, studying their routines and waiting for the right opportunity to strike. The alternative theory argued that he scouted locations instead. According to this view, he selected secluded spots that ensured minimal risk, then attacked whichever couple happened to be there. A more complex version of this theory suggested that both elements were at play: he might follow certain victims until learning where they habitually went to be alone, then he prepared his assault accordingly.

The timing of the murders also generated speculation. The Monster struck almost exclusively on weekends. One explanation was practical: weekends were when most couples went out at night and sought privacy. Another interpretation was psychological: perhaps the killer had a weekday job, a stable occupation that structured his life and limited his opportunities to kill. But again, this could have been mere coincidence. A serial killer might simply take advantage of the behavioral patterns of his targets rather than follow a personal calendar.

As investigators analyzed the growing number of homicides, they noticed a series of troubling coincidences among the victims:

- **Many of the Italian victims had recently lost a parent.**
  This struck investigators as unusual. Was the killer

selecting people during emotionally fragile periods? Or was it merely chance?

- **All of the victims belonged to lower social classes.**
  Not a single murder involved a couple from a higher socioeconomic background. This raised questions about accessibility, visibility, and the killer's familiarity with certain social groups.

- **Every couple was in a committed relationship.**
  Despite the widespread infidelity characteristic of rural Italy at the time, no clandestine lovers, adulterous couples, or one-night affairs were ever targeted. This reinforced the idea that the Monster might follow predictable, "clean" patterns—stable couples with regular habits.

- **Many of the female victims had previously reported being followed or approached by strange men.**
  Several had noticed unsettling behavior in the days or weeks before their deaths, suggesting that the killer may have been monitoring them.

- **A striking number of victims worked in the textile industry.**
  Tuscany had a large textile sector, so this connection might simply reflect demographics— but investigators took note, wondering whether the killer encountered victims through professional channels.

In 1984, in an effort to bring order to the chaos, Professor Francesco De Fazio, one of

Italy's leading criminologists, was asked to produce a psychological profile of the Monster. At the time, profiling was still in its infancy in Italy, but De Fazio drew on international studies of serial offenders.

According to his preliminary report, the Monster was likely a solitary male of Anglo-Saxon physical type, between 30 and 40 years old, approximately 1.80 meters tall. De Fazio theorized that the killer suffered from sexual deviations and murdered out of lust, driven by internal impulses rather than external triggers.

This profile inspired several investigative theories, many of which shaped the public debate for years. Among those who drew from De Fazio's perspective were lawyer Nino Filastò, journalist Mario Spezi, and American writer Douglas Preston.

Filastò, analyzing the crime scenes, argued that specific clues pointed toward a killer who could approach couples without raising suspicion. The silence of the victims, the absence of defensive wounds in some cases, and the consistent attack positions suggested a man who inspired either trust or fear. Filastò also noted that certain personal documents—wallets, licenses, circulation permits—were found oddly displaced. To him, this hinted at a killer who might be a uniformed officer or someone impersonating one. A man approaching a parked car late at night in a remote area might be obeyed if mistaken for law enforcement.

Mario Spezi, among the first journalists to investigate the crimes, gave the killer his infamous label: *Il Mostro di Firenze*. Spezi believed that the key to the entire case lay in a single object: the gun. He insisted that the Beretta .22 used in the 1968 murder was the same weapon used in all subsequent homicides from 1974 onward. The ballistic match, in his view, was undeniable.

Spezi argued that because the gun was linked to the Sardinian clan involved in the 1968 case, and because firearms used in underworld murders are never willingly passed on, the weapon must have remained in the hands of someone connected to that first homicide. He theorized that the gun had eventually been stolen—a rare but possible event—and used again by the real Monster.

Spezi and Douglas Preston meticulously traced the weapon's history, building a timeline of its movements and proposing that the Monster was a marginal member of the Sardinian group— someone overlooked in previous investigations and conveniently absent from Tuscany during periods when no murders occurred.

Their theory, though controversial, became one of the most widely discussed interpretations of the case.

And so, over the years, the Monster of Florence investigation became not just a manhunt, but a complex labyrinth of competing theories—medical, geographic, psychological, sociological, and conspiratorial. Each tried to impose order on a pattern of violence that resisted explanation. Each revealed different fears, cultural blind spots, and investigative limitations.

Yet despite the debates, disagreements, and thousands of pages written, one thing remains clear: the Monster always stayed one step ahead, not because he was invisible, but because every attempt to understand him only deepened the mystery.

Composite sketch created from several witness statements, which later became the starting point for the so-called "Redhead of Mugello" theory, a theory that was definitively dismissed by the Florence Prosecutor's Office in 2025.

Another composite sketch of the alleged killer, based on the statements of Bardazzi, a bartender who in 1984 noticed a suspicious person who, according to him, was watching Pia Rontini and Claudio Stefanacci.

R.59635.

Grafico di persona da identi=
ficare (duplice omicidio BAL=
DI — CAMBI)Calenzano 23.10.81
ETA 45-55/CORP. REGOLARE/SPAL=
LE LARGHE/COLORITO BRUNO/CAPEL=
LI E OCCHI SGURI.----------------

The most infamous composite sketch of the
Monster of Florence.

THE SARDINIAN LEAD

The term "Sardinian Lead" refers to the long and complex branch of the Monster of Florence investigations that focused on the so-called Sardinian clan. Over the years, a large number of individuals connected directly or indirectly to this group were questioned, accused, or placed under surveillance. Many of them had criminal records, turbulent personal histories, or reputations that attracted suspicion. Their behavior toward the authorities was often provocative, uncooperative, or inconsistent, which further fueled investigative attention.

For a time, this line of inquiry appeared promising. Investigators believed that the origins of the crimes might be tied to the 1968 homicide involving Barbara Locci and Antonio Lo Bianco, a case in which several Sardinians were implicated. As a result, the idea that the Monster emerged from within that same circle gained traction. Various suspects were arrested, interrogated, and detained. But each time, the Monster struck again while one or more of these individuals were in jail, systematically disproving the accusations.

Despite the volume of suspects and the intense scrutiny, no concrete evidence ever connected any member of the Sardinian group to the later murders. In this sense, the theory later developed by Mario Spezi and Douglas Preston can be seen as an extension of the same investigative path. Ultimately, the Sardinian Lead was officially abandoned in 1989, leaving behind years of frustration and unanswered questions.

Giovanni Mele and Pietro Mucciarini.

Francisco Vinci and Salvatore Vinci.

Avete visto quest'uomo?

I carabinieri tirano fuori dagli archivi
l'identikit di un uomo visto a Calenzano poco
dopo il penultimo omicidio del «mostro»
Ma potrebbe anche essere solo un testimone

Italian newspapers from the time reporting on the
case.

Vinci compare in aula
«Non sono il mostro»

La sfida del mostro

Prima firma il delitto sparando dietro l'orecchio sinistro
poi martirizza entrambi i cadaveri con raffinata ferocia

Massimo
allarme
Massimo
impegno

CRONACA Nei dintorni di Firenze si aggira un assassino che ha già trucidato...

C'È UN MOSTRO CHE ODIA CHI SI AMA

Esce dal buio della notte. Si avventa alle auto degli innamorati, spara e mutila il corpo delle ragazze. Poi sparisce nel nulla. Pare un film dell'orrore ma è magica realtà. Un incubo che dura ormai da anni anni.

di Alberto Bevilacqua

CelliLino   cambival

firenze

879.202 - 663.663

Perché sono stati arrestati il fratello e il cognato di Stefano Mele

La clamorosa svolta «Prove inequivocabili»

In un biglietto la verità sul '68?
Ma la «calibro 22» resta nel buio

di ALESSANDRO FIESOLI

PIETRO PACCIANI

In 1992, Ruggero Perugini, the leader of the so-called Anti-Monster Team—a special unit made up of police officers and carabinieri dedicated exclusively to the case—did something unprecedented. During a televised broadcast on RAI, he took the microphone and launched a direct appeal to the Monster. Looking back today, the scene still carries an air of professional desperation mixed with fierce determination. Perugini wasn't speaking to viewers, nor to the press. He was speaking to him—the Monster— almost as if he truly believed the killer might be watching at that very moment.

«I don't know why, but I have the feeling that at this moment you are watching me, so listen. People here call you Monster, maniac, animal, but in these years I think I learned to know you and maybe to understand you, and I know that you are only the poor slave of an old nightmare that governs you.

You are not crazy as people say, your fantasies, your impulses have taken you hand and govern your actions.

I know that even in this moment you are trying to fight against them. We want you to know that we will help you overcome them.

I know that the past taught you suspicion and silence, but in this moment, I am not lying to you and never will, if you decide to free yourself from this monster who tyrannizes you. You know how, when, and where to find me. I will be waiting for you.»

Those words—broadcast live across the country—revealed much about the state of mind of the investigators at the time. After almost twenty years of dead ends, false trails, misleading clues, public pressure, and murders that continued despite arrests and interrogations, the authorities believed they were finally close to the truth.

They were convinced the Monster now had a name: Pietro Pacciani.

And the image of this man clashed with every profile drawn up until that moment. He was not tall, not educated, not refined. He was not a doctor, a hunter, or a technician. Instead, he was a small, rough Tuscan farmer with a history of domestic violence and sexual abuse. A man living on the margins of society, someone who hardly resembled the ritualistic, organized serial killer imagined by experts.

To understand how investigators reached him, we need to go back a few years.

Pacciani first came under suspicion on September 11, 1985, the day after the Monster's final double homicide, the one at Scopeti. An anonymous letter had been delivered to the authorities identifying him as a potential suspect. Much later, it would be revealed that the letter came from a fellow villager who simply disliked him and had personal, unfounded suspicions.

Despite this weak lead, the police carried out a search of his home. They found nothing of interest, and for some time Pacciani remained a marginal figure in the investigation. But when the Anti-Monster Team was created, things began to shift. Perugini and his unit compiled several lists of potential suspects based on age, residence, criminal history, and other parameters. With each revision, the lists grew shorter, yet Pacciani's name always remained.

Investigators found his past particularly significant. In the 1950s, Pacciani had been convicted of the murder of a man he found with his girlfriend. According to the court reconstruction, after stabbing the rival to death, he forced the young woman to have sex with him next to the body. Over the years, Pacciani had accumulated a long record of domestic violence and had even served time for sexually abusing his own daughters. Without any doubt, he was a violent man. But was he the Monster of Florence?

Between 1990 and 1992, police searched his home multiple times. During these searches, they found several objects the prosecution considered "compromising," including:

• newspaper clippings showing women's breasts

• a road map with Signa and San Casciano circled

• a painting depicting a figure in uniform

• a sign for mediumistic séances and other occult objects

• a pair of working binoculars

• a 1985 flyer with a Florentine license plate and the word "couple" written on the back

- a notebook with the note: "Vicchio–Mercatale 132 kilometers"

- a sheet of paper with the date of the Scopeti murder

- newspaper clippings about the Monster

- a defective Winchester H-series .22 caliber cartridge

- a "Skizzen Brunner" sketchbook sold exclusively in Germany and a German-made soap dish

For the prosecution, these items formed a psychological and environmental tapestry pointing toward a man obsessed with the killings. For the defense, they were a mix of ambiguous, unrelated objects that held no direct evidentiary value. None of them, examined individually, placed Pacciani at any of the crime scenes.

Nevertheless, in 1993, Pacciani was arrested and formally charged as the Monster of Florence.

During his trial, prosecutors relied heavily on recordings obtained from hidden microphones placed inside his home. These tapes revealed a household riddled with violence. Pacciani insulted, threatened, and assaulted his wife for seemingly trivial reasons. But even this extensive surveillance failed to capture any direct reference to the murders.

One intercepted conversation became particularly notorious. After police interrogated his wife Angiolina—during which she admitted that Pacciani had once owned a firearm—he became enraged. He had instructed her beforehand to claim she had a headache and did not want to speak. Her cooperation with investigators infuriated him, and he assaulted her. She fled the home.

Alone in the house afterward, unaware he was being monitored, Pacciani moved around the kitchen. At one point he muttered something that investigators interpreted as:

«Where do I put it now?»

To the prosecution, "it" was the gun. To the defense, "it" referred to some other object, especially since in Italian the word "gun" is feminine, while Pacciani used the masculine pronoun. Some theorists—stretching the possibility further—suggested he was referring to an audio or video tape containing recordings related to the murders, potentially used for blackmail. But no recordings were ever found, and no solid evidence supported such claims. Most likely, these were imaginative interpretations.

A more serious question arose: if investigators believed he was talking about the murder weapon, why didn't they intervene immediately? Their failure to act became yet another controversial gray area in the case.

Pacciani's financial situation added further suspicion. For someone who lived off small jobs and had spent years in prison, he appeared to possess an unusual amount of money—equivalent to several hundred thousand euros today. Some postal voucher transactions were dated close to certain murders. Investigators speculated that the money could have come from blackmail or payment for contract killings.

However, in Italy during the 1970s and 1980s, under-the-table labor was extremely common. It is entirely possible that Pacciani earned the money legally but off the books. Still, the doubts persisted.

In 1994, Pacciani was convicted in the first trial. But the ruling included a surprising note: for the last homicide—the killing of the French couple in Scopeti—there may have been two killers. If true, this implied that Pacciani had an accomplice.

As the appeal trial began in 1996, the case quickly began to unravel. The weaknesses of the prosecution's arguments became obvious. The evidence was thin, circumstantial, and often contradicted by other findings. The testimonies lacked consistency. The material seized during the searches did not establish guilt.

After only a few days, the unthinkable occurred: the prosecution itself requested Pacciani's acquittal.

He was released and walked out of the courtroom a free man.

During the final session of the appeal, the prosecution attempted a dramatic move: they introduced four new alleged witnesses, referred to only by Greek letters—Alpha, Beta, Gamma, and Delta. Due to procedural rules, the testimony was not admitted. With that, the trial concluded.

However, the case was far from closed. Later in 1996, the Italian Supreme Court annulled the acquittal and ordered a new trial. Pacciani would have returned to court, still under suspicion.

But he never made it.

On February 22, 1998, Pietro Pacciani was found dead in his home in Mercatale. The official cause: a heart attack. Yet the circumstances raised immediate questions. His body was discovered with his pants pulled down and his sweater lifted. Toxicology reports revealed traces of a powerful asthma medication—one known to be extremely dangerous for someone with his cardiac conditions.

Two possibilities emerged:

• He took the drug accidentally, unaware of the risks.

• Someone administered it to him.

No definitive conclusion was ever reached.

On that day, the curtain fell on the life of Pietro Pacciani. With his death, the judicial battle surrounding him ended forever. And yet, the true Monster of Florence—the real killer—remained in the shadows, unidentified, untouched, and still haunting the Tuscan countryside.

Pietro Pacciani at the time of his first arrest in 1951, for the Tassinaia murder.

Pietro Pacciani in the 1950s.

Pietro Pacciani in the 1980s.

Pietro Pacciani with his daughters in the 1980s.
Pacciani was convicted in 1987 for sexually assaulting
his daughters.

Pietro Pacciani in the courtroom during the trials for the Monster of Florence murders.

Pietro Pacciani in the 1990s.

The envelope of the infamous anonymous letter sent
by the Monster of Florence to Della Monica in 1985.

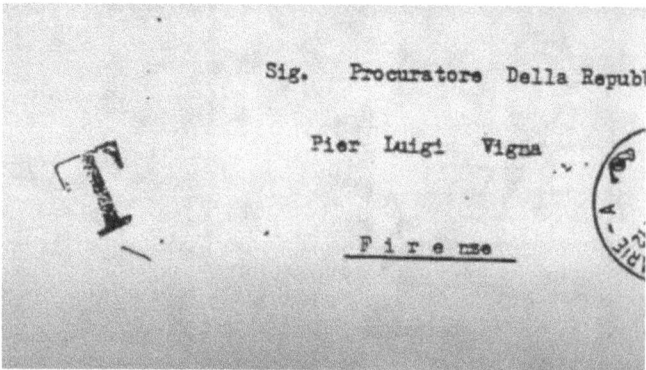

The envelope of the anonymous letter sent by the
Monster of Florence to Pier Luigi Vigna.

The shell casing found in Pacciani's garden. In 2025, after Ruggero Perugini's death, it emerged that this casing had been fabricated by the prosecutor's office to frame Pacciani.

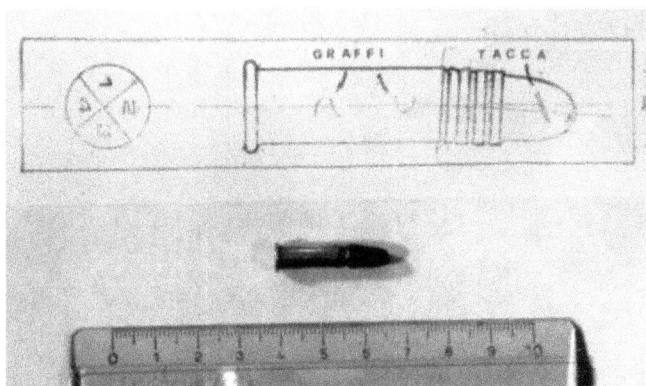

THE "PICNICKING FRIENDS"

The expression *"picnicking friends"* first appeared during the initial trial of Pietro Pacciani. It emerged almost by accident, yet it would eventually come to define one of the most controversial chapters in the entire Monster of Florence investigation. Among the many witnesses called to testify was Mario Vanni, a longtime acquaintance of Pacciani and, at the time, the mailman of their small Tuscan village. When Vanni took the stand, the judge asked him a routine question: "Mister Vanni, what is your occupation?" His answer was as unusual as it was revealing. Instead of simply stating his profession, he blurted out, "I have been hanging out with Pacciani sometime having a picnic." The awkward phrasing suggested rehearsed lines, as though someone had coached him on what to say and he had mixed up his answers.

From that instant forward, investigators and the media began referring to Pacciani and his closest companions as "the picnicking friends," a nickname that came to symbolize a group of rural outcasts, simple men drawn into a vortex of accusations far beyond their understanding.

But who exactly were the picnicking friends according to the prosecution? And how did investigators arrive at the idea that Pacciani did not act alone?

To answer this, we must return to the moment when prosecutors attempted to introduce four new witnesses during Pacciani's second trial—witnesses identified only by the Greek letters Alpha, Beta, Gamma, and Delta. Their real names were Fernando Pucci, Giancarlo Lotti, Gabriella Ghiribelli, and Norberto Galli. These individuals emerged from a combination of wiretaps, informal conversations, and local inquiries conducted among Pacciani's circle. After years of searching for unknown clues, investigators suddenly had a new lead from within the very community where many of the crimes occurred.

The 1994 verdict had already suggested that the murders might involve more than one killer. The possibility of accomplices seemed increasingly plausible, especially since the murder weapon—the famous .22 caliber Beretta—had never been found. The theory was that someone local might still be hiding it.

One of the wiretapped conversations proved especially explosive. In a phone call between Giancarlo Lotti and Gabriella Ghiribelli, Lotti hinted that he had witnessed the last murder, the 1985 killing of the French couple. The implication was enormous. When investigators brought him in for questioning, Lotti initially denied everything. But after hours of inconsistencies, contradictions, and confused statements, he eventually broke down and confessed.

Lotti claimed he had been present at the crime scene during the murder of the French couple, not as an active participant but as a lookout. According to his confession, Pacciani and Vanni carried out the killings and removed the body parts—the so-called "fetishes"—while he kept watch. Lotti also insisted that he had brought along a friend, Fernando Pucci, a man with significant cognitive delays. He claimed Pucci had nothing to do with the murders and had not participated in any violence.

Ghiribelli and Galli, the other two individuals identified by Greek letters in the prosecution's earlier attempt, added fuel to the fire. They confirmed that, on the night of the French couple's murder, they had driven near the spot where the victims were parked—and had seen Lotti's car in the area. To investigators hungry for leads, this sounded like corroboration.

Lotti, once he began confessing, became a flood of stories. He not only described the events at Scopeti but claimed he was also present at the Vicchio double murder. He even said he heard Pia screaming as Pacciani pulled her from the car. Yet this detail immediately clashed with forensic findings. According to the autopsy, Pia had been fatally shot early in the attack and had lost consciousness almost instantly. She could not have screamed, struggled, or reacted during the mutilation. It was medically impossible.

This contradiction highlighted a larger issue: Lotti was an alcoholic with significant cognitive impairment, prone to confusion and highly susceptible to suggestion. Yet his confession became the cornerstone of what prosecutors called the "picnicking friends" theory.

The trial that followed exposed an unsettling world beneath the quiet surface of rural Tuscany. While Pacciani's own trial had revealed a household marked by violence and abuse, the picnicking friends trial opened a wider window onto the darker corners of provincial life—areas previously whispered about but seldom addressed openly.

The courtroom heard accounts of prostitution, sexual perversions, voyeurism, and ritualistic practices rooted in old local folklore. There were mentions of black magic, superstitions, and improvised occult ceremonies —behaviors that painted a picture of a community struggling with poverty, ignorance, and long-standing cultural taboos. The trial brought these secrets out into the open, sensationalized by the press and magnified by the public's hunger for a monstrous explanation.

According to the official reconstruction presented in court, Pacciani, Vanni, and at times Lotti were responsible for at least the last four murders attributed to the Monster of Florence. But the prosecution did not stop there. Lotti introduced an additional, shocking element: according to him, the trio acted on the orders of an unidentified gentleman of high social standing —a doctor, a prominent figure—who supposedly commissioned the murders and paid them in exchange for the mutilated body parts.

This notion suggested a mastermind, a member of an elite circle, someone untouchable. It implied the existence of a broader network of participants motivated by occult or esoteric beliefs, willing to pay desperate rural men to kill and retrieve anatomical trophies.

The claim echoed the long-standing Italian fascination with conspiracies involving powerful hidden figures—the sort of narrative that thrives when fear meets uncertainty. For the prosecution, this was a possible explanation for the money that both Pacciani and Vanni possessed at the time of their arrests—sums difficult to reconcile with their modest incomes as a farmhand and a mailman.

Indeed, like Pacciani, Mario Vanni also had a surprising amount of money saved, far more than what one would expect from a postal worker living in a small Tuscan village. To investigators eager for answers, this seemed to support Lotti's claim of payments from a mysterious benefactor.

And yet, the entire structure of the picnicking friends theory rested on statements made by deeply unreliable witnesses. There was no physical evidence connecting Lotti or Vanni to any murder scene. No fingerprints, no DNA, no ballistics, no fibers, no tools, no weapons. The accusations were built almost entirely on Lotti's confused, contradictory confessions—stories that repeatedly clashed with irrefutable forensic facts.

Still, in a case where every lead had collapsed over decades, investigators pushed forward with what they had.

The picnicking friends trial became another chapter in the long, tragic, and often absurd history of the Monster of Florence investigations —a blend of rural desperation, investigative frustration, and the human tendency to seek meaning where truth remains elusive. Whether these men were hapless bystanders caught in a hurricane of suspicion, or whether they knew more than they ever revealed, remains one of the many unresolved mysteries in a saga marked by unanswered questions.

Otto vittime, una sola firma

Esiste da mesi, ormai, un ritratto psicologico dell'omicida, ma le indagini non sembrano progredire

Le prime testimonianze
«Lui era al volante...»
«No, era dietro»

I due ragazzi uccisi
Sempre insieme
dopo il lavoro

Il parere di uno psichiatra
Il 'mostro' è in mezzo a noi
Riconoscerlo è impossibile

Italian newspapers from the time reporting on the case.

Un uomo si è costituito ai CC: «Carmela e Giovanni li ho uccisi io»

Assassino o mitomane?

Ha 40 anni e abita a Scandicci - Ora dove far ritrovare la pistola calibro 22

DI RICCARDO CATOLA

Senza risultato l'incontro in comune

Sesto interrogatorio per Guido Niccolai

E' certo: uno solo l'autore dei tre spaventosi delitti

L'incubo del mostro - assassino di notte nella periferia di Firenze

L'autista della Misericordia Enzo Spalletti scarcerato

Spadolini anticipa a domani l'incontro coi sindacati

L'assassino colpirà ancora
DI ENNIO MACCONI

Perchè è libero il «guardone»
DI FRANCA SELVATICI

Italian newspapers from the time reporting on the case.

Italian newspapers from the time reporting on the case.

Non esistono prove concrete della colpevolezza di Spalletti

Così fu trovato la mattina di domenica sette giugno il corpo di Carmela di Nuccio

(testo dell'articolo in gran parte illeggibile)

Alessandro Cecioni

Italian newspapers from the time reporting on the case.

THE MASTERMINDS AND FRANCESCO NARDUCCI

The investigation grows more and more complicated. Every time it seems the last piece of the puzzle has finally been found, the picture changes shape. Instead of a clear image, investigators are left with shifting outlines and new shadows.

In the years after the trials of Pietro Pacciani and the so-called "picnicking friends," one theory takes hold inside a part of the investigative world. According to this view, three grotesque and marginal figures like Pacciani, Vanni, and Lotti could not have engineered such a long and brutal series of murders on their own. They might have carried out the killings, but they would have done so under the influence, or under the orders, of an external power.

That power, as imagined by some investigators, would be a hidden group of powerful individuals, people "beyond suspicion," shielded by their professions, social standing, and prominent family names. Behind the polite façade of status and respectability, these people would have directed the crimes, using men like Pacciani and his circle as tools. The motive, in this theory, is esoteric. The murders would have been commissioned for ritual purposes, for some form of occult or magical objective.

From this point of view, the crimes of the Monster of Florence are not the acts of a lone sexual sadist but the visible surface of a darker, organized project. The mutilations, the removal of body parts, the choice of locations, the timing of the attacks, everything is read through an esoteric lens.

According to this school of thought, there are what they call "obvious signs" of ritual and black magic in the murders.

First, the same weapon was used in all the crimes. For a traditional criminal investigation this is a normal indication of a serial killer. For those leaning toward an esoteric explanation, it is framed as a ritual constant, a "consecrated" object used repeatedly, as in certain occult practices where the same knife or tool is used for each sacrifice.

Second, the murders all take place on moonless nights. To an investigator driven by this type of reading, the absence of moonlight is not just a tactical advantage that provides darkness and cover. It becomes a symbolic choice. Moonless nights are associated, in some occult circles, with certain rituals, invocations, or negative energies.

Third, the locations of the murders. The crime scenes are often in areas near woods, fields, or watercourses. In the esoteric theory, these natural elements are not just part of the Tuscan landscape. They are loaded with symbolic value. Trees, crossroads, and running water have been associated with magic, transitions, and offerings in many traditions. The fact that couples are killed in rural, liminal spaces, close to woods and near water, is seen as further confirmation of ritual meaning.

Then there are the physical clues found at or near the crime scenes.

In 1981, near the scene of the Bartoline homicide, investigators discover a pyramidal black basalt stone, shaped like a truncated cone. For some, this stone is an esoteric totem, a small altar, or a symbol placed there with intention. For others, it is nothing more than a decorative object, possibly a door knob or a piece of garden hardware that ended up in the area for entirely mundane reasons.

In another case, near the spot where the French couple had camped a few days before their murder, a gamekeeper finds a series of stones arranged in circular patterns. They are ring-shaped designs on the ground. He removes them, but later reports what he saw. For certain self-styled esoteric experts consulted by the investigators, these stone circles represent nothing less than a symbolic portrait of the French couple, pre-selected and marked for sacrifice. In this reading, the stones are not random. They are a sign that the victims were chosen in advance.

To someone skeptical, all of this sounds fragile and speculative. But within the world of the investigation, especially during moments of frustration and deadlock, such theories gain traction.

In reality, the esoteric theory is not entirely new. It had been proposed years earlier by criminologist Francesco Bruno, who in 1984 wrote a profile of the killer at the request of the Italian secret services. In that report, often referred to as "the Bruno file," he suggested that the killer was driven by mystical and esoteric impulses. However, the document is said to have vanished. According to what is known today, it never reached the desks of the investigators working directly on the Monster case.

Bruno, working together with his wife Simonetta Costanzo, developed an interpretation in which the mystic and esoteric aspect is rooted in the killer's own psychology, not in a structured satanic cult. For them, the ritual element comes from inside the murderer's mind, from his unconscious drives, fantasies, and symbolic compulsions. It has more to do with his inner world than with a planned series of homicides coordinated by an organized group. In other words, the esotericism is individual and psychological, not social and conspiratorial.

The later "sect" theory that emerges around Pacciani and the picnicking friends flips that idea completely. Now the ritual is framed as collective and premeditated, not as a private obsession. Under this theory, the Monster is not acting alone. He is obeying orders.

The natural question then becomes: who are these supposed members of the esoteric sect beyond suspicion?

Rumors and names circulate for years. The image is always the same. "Big shots." Important people. Professionals with degrees, titles, and influence. Men whose social masks would make them untouchable. At different times, some of these names even end up in official documents or in the media.

One of the people dragged into this orbit is Francesco Calamandrei, a pharmacist from San Casciano. He finds himself on the defendant's bench, accused in connection with the Monster case. After a long process, he is fully acquitted. The accusations collapse for lack of evidence. Still, his name remains associated, in the public imagination, with the idea of a powerful provincial figure mixed up in dark events.

The most notorious name, however, comes back into focus through a wiretap that, at least at first, has nothing to do with the Monster. In the recording, a woman who is a victim of loan-sharking is being threatened over the phone. The man on the other end tells her that if she does not behave, he will *"finish her off like the doctor found in Lake Trasimeno."*

That phrase—"the doctor found in Lake Trasimeno"—immediately catches the attention of investigators.

Who is this doctor?

At first glance, the reference seems to point to Francesco Narducci, a gastrointestinal specialist from Perugia who died in 1985 in the waters of Lake Trasimeno. Yet a more precise interpretation could suggest another name: Giampiero Puletti, a doctor involved in a usury case who died by suicide on the shores of Lake Trasimeno in 1995. The wording of the threat could be read either way.

But it is the name Narducci that slowly becomes entangled, in public debate and in some investigative circles, with the Monster of Florence.

Who was Francesco Narducci, and what do we know about him?

He was from Perugia, part of a prominent local family deeply rooted in the city's professional and social life. He worked as a gastrointestinal specialist and enjoyed a comfortable, even enviable lifestyle. By all accounts he was very wealthy. He had married Francesca Spagnoli, herself from a well-known family. On paper, it looked like the picture of success in a provincial Italian city: a respected doctor, a good marriage, economic security, social standing.

Everything about Narducci appears completely normal. Nothing in his official biography suggests deviance or violence. The only detail that stands out slightly is that he owned a gun. In itself, that was not unusual in Italy in those years, especially among hunters or people who liked to keep a handgun.

Yet despite the apparently unremarkable life, rumors about him begin to circulate as early as the 1980s. A local vox populi, a whisper passed from mouth to mouth, links his name to the Monster story. According to some sources, the Anti-Monster Team itself had him on a list of highly suspicious individuals during those years.

We do not know exactly what led investigators toward Narducci back then. There must have been some reason, but the documentation is thin and fragmented. Perhaps it was an anonymous letter—hundreds were sent during the height of the investigation. Perhaps it was a comment made by someone in the medical environment. Perhaps it was a local rumor that reached the wrong ears at the right moment.

There are mentions of a nurse from Foligno who supposedly reported something unusual connected to him. There are stories that his car or motorcycle was seen near one of the crime scenes on the night of a murder. Another version claims that his motorcycle forced its way through a police roadblock a few days before his disappearance. There are also rumors of checks and inquiries carried out by law enforcement in an entirely unofficial way, leaving almost no formal trace.

These are fragments. Voices. Memories. Put together, they form a suggestive picture, but not a solid one. Over time they are repeated, reshaped, and passed along, while the number of written documents remains small.

What is certain is that Narducci died in 1985, shortly after the double murder of the French couple. The official version says it was an accident at the lake. The timing, however, is striking. He dies exactly when, according to some, the investigation was closing in on him.

From that moment onward, the investigation, as we know, takes a different direction. One practical reason is that it comes out that, during the Calenzano murder of 1981, Narducci was enrolled in a specialization course in the United States. For some, this functions as an alibi. But the course did not require mandatory attendance, and there are no detailed records proving his physical presence in America at the exact time of the murder. The uncertainty remains.

The fact that this lead was essentially abandoned between 1985 and 2002 leaves a lingering sense of unease. People who later review the case cannot help but ask whether an important track was dropped too quickly.

The story of Narducci's death is filled with gray zones and contradictions, especially concerning what happened on October 8, 1985, the day he disappeared.

According to the official reconstruction, that morning Narducci is at work at the Monteluce hospital in Perugia. At some point he receives a phone call. After answering, he tells colleagues he needs to leave. He returns home, has lunch with his wife, and then decides to go to the lake for a boat ride. Before getting on the water, he reportedly stops at a family property in San Feliciano, near the lake, where he leaves a written message. The content of that note is often described but rarely cited in full in public sources.

He then gets into a boat and disappears.

A few hours later, search and rescue teams find the boat empty, floating on the water. No trace of Narducci is found. For days, divers and boats search the lake. Finally, on October 13, a body surfaces from the depths. It is identified as his.

Here the case takes a new and disturbing turn.

The Narducci family is well known and powerful in Perugia. Some observers argue that this status helped accelerate the bureaucratic procedures and simplify the handling of the case. In practice, what this means is that the investigation into his death is not conducted with the same rigor that would be expected in similar circumstances.

The cause of death remains uncertain, and no autopsy is performed at the time. The body is quickly buried. Officials accept drowning as the most plausible explanation, and the file is effectively closed.

Yet not everyone is convinced. Some people claim that the body pulled from the lake that day did not look like Francesco Narducci at all.

They describe a corpse that is too swollen, too dark, with hair that appears different from his. The body is in an advanced state of decomposition, out of proportion to the fact that he had disappeared only a few days earlier. Most striking of all, they insist that the man lying on the pier is significantly shorter than Narducci.

Supporting these doubts are the testimonies of various witnesses and a set of "stolen" photographs taken during the recovery operation. Police had cordoned off the pier, blocking access and attempting to keep journalists and photographers away. At some point, however, someone manages to find an angle and shoot photos of the body laid out on the dock.

The images are taken from a distance, at an angle that does not allow a clear view of the face.

Even so, certain details are visible. The crime scene unit of the carabinieri studies the photos and compares the corpse's height to the regular spacing of the wooden planks on the pier. From this, they estimate that the body recovered from the lake is at least 10 to 15 centimeters shorter than Narducci.

This is not proof, but it is enough to raise serious questions.

In 2002, the body in Narducci's grave is exhumed. This time, a full autopsy is performed. Experts determine without any doubt that the body in the coffin is in fact that of Francesco Narducci. So the man buried there is him.

Yet that does not completely resolve the earlier doubts. The condition of the corpse in 2002 does not match the description of the decomposed, misshapen body seen on the pier in 1985. The body in the coffin is in relatively good condition, compatible with slow decomposition in a sealed casket. Many witnesses insist that the body they saw in 1985 was much more deteriorated.

The autopsy yields another shock. It concludes that the cause of death was not drowning, and that his body did not appear to have been in water for five days. On an old corpse, such assessments are not always exact, but the indication is strong enough to cast doubt on the original story of a simple boating accident.

Even more troubling, the pathologists note lesions on the thyroid cartilage, injuries that are compatible with strangulation. In other words, there are signs that his neck was compressed by external force.

If this is true, then Narducci did not die in the lake. He was killed in some other way and then, at some point, associated with the lake through a staged narrative.

In 2010, after years of media coverage and judicial back-and-forth, the Prosecutor's Office in Perugia brings charges against 19 individuals accused of participating in a staged recovery of the body at the lake and a subsequent cover-up. On April 20, 2010, at the end of the preliminary hearing, all are acquitted. The case, at least on a judicial level, closes. Officially, there is no proof of a conspiracy.

Yet doubts remain. Many observers cannot ignore the mysterious coincidences surrounding Narducci. The double murder of the French couple is the last known homicide of the Monster. The killings stop after his death or after his disappearance, depending on which version one believes. His name had supposedly appeared on suspect lists in earlier years. His financial status and social connections placed him in a world far removed from the peasants and marginal figures who had occupied the spotlight in previous trials.

But is this enough to call him the Monster?

If he were the Monster, he would fit the profile drawn by many criminologists: a lone serial killer, intelligent, educated, with a respectable facade and a double life. That image clashes with the figure of Pacciani and the picnicking friends. What role would they then play in the story? Were they supposed to be accomplices, fall guys, or something else entirely?

How can we realistically link their primitive and violent lifestyle, their drunken evenings, their brutal and almost illiterate existence, to the refined, professional, and socially sophisticated environment of a doctor from high society? How do we bridge the gap between rural bars and medical conferences, between mud and marble?

And what about the esoteric sect? Does it really exist? Could a large organization of wealthy occultists have operated for years, ordering crimes, paying killers, and influencing investigations, all while remaining invisible? Could they have diverted attention away from Narducci, if he was indeed part of their circle?

These are questions. Hypotheses. Sometimes they feel closer to pure fantasy than to investigative reasoning. Still, for many, Narducci appears to be the perfect missing piece—the figure that would finally align the early criminal profiles with an actual suspect. Here, at last, would be someone with Anglo-Saxon features, a sophisticated education, and a professional background that matches the theoretical image of the Monster crafted in psychological reports over the years. All the characteristics that were missing in Spalletti, in Vinci, in Pacciani, in Lotti, in Vanni, and in all the other grotesque characters who populated the investigation seem to converge in him.

And yet, even here, the puzzle does not truly close.

Because when we put all the pieces together, we see that we are trying to force connections between people, environments, and situations that often have little or nothing in common. The story of Narducci is suspicious and mysterious, just as the stories of many others who have crossed, even briefly, the path of this case are suspicious and mysterious.

Digging into their lives has revealed worlds and situations we might prefer not to know existed: violence within families, illegal dealings, contempt for institutions, and constant small abuses of power. These are monstrous realities. But none of them, at least so far, has allowed anyone to write a definitive final line to this story.

The case of the Monster of Florence remains, in every sense, an indecipherable puzzle.

Every time someone claims to have solved it, to have found the key that explains everything, it eventually becomes clear that some pieces were forced into place, or that other pieces were left unused. The image that appears in front of us is always incomplete, always distorted. And when that realization comes, we have no choice but to go back to the beginning, pick up the pieces again, and admit that the picture is still not clear.

cronaca

679.202 - 663.663

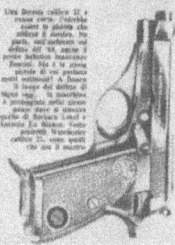

Viaggio sulle tracce della calibro 22 che il mostro usa per uccidere (1)

L'arma che tutti videro ma che nessuno trovò

Italian newspapers from the time reporting on the case.

Francesco Narducci.

The pier on Lake Trasimeno where the body of
Francesco Narducci was recovered.

Francesco Narducci.

Francesco Narducci.

Francesco Narducci.

INTERVIEW
WITH PAOLO COCHI[1]

The following is an exclusive interview with director and filmmaker Paolo Cochi, the author of the popular documentary "The murders of the Monster of Florence". Cochi is considered one of the most knowledgeable researchers about the case.

To this day, it is still not clear how the police came to link the 1968 case to the series of murders committed by the Monster of Florence: was it because of anonymous letters mailed to the

[1] Interview conducted in 2012 on the occasion of the launch of the audiobook "The Monster of Florence" by Jacopo Pezzan and Giacomo Brunoro

carabinieri or Marshal Fiori's remembrance? If the correct answer is anonymous letters, then how many were there and what did they say?

According to the journalist Mario Spezi and the lawyer Filastò, General Tricomi received an envelope containing a cut-out of the newspaper article about the 1968 murder reading: "why don't you take a closer look at the 1968 trial back in Perugia's tribunal". This recount has never been refuted and it seems that Marshal Fiori had no involvement in the investigation of the 1968 Signa murder.

During our research, we came across a chain of worrisome coincidences linking the Italian victims to one another. We are referring to that fact that many of those victims worked in the textile industry and that many had recently lost a relative. The most unexpected finding was that the Monster,, with the exception of the 1968 murder, did not shoot couples of clandestine lovers who most certainly must have been around during those years; practically all the victims were in a committed relationship and came from a low social background. Not one victim was the son or daughter of a high ranked professional. How do you explain it? Are these all mere coincidences or is it possible to draw a profile of the Monster based on these elements?

In my thought process, the killer had some sort of fanatic sense of justice with a religious touch. In two of the murders (1968 and 1984), the Monster ripped the necklaces with a cross pendant from the victims' necks.I believe that the Monster's targeting couples in their vehicles, in the midst of an intimate act away from the marital nest is a significant element in determining his personality. As for the victims' social background, I thinks that it is probably a coincidence linked to the fact that these young victims have less economic resources that would allow them to afford a motel room or a private home for their sexual activities.With regard to the clandestine couples, I suppose that the chances of finding a clandestine couple on a Friday or Saturday evening during summer are somewhat slim.

One of the most debated elements in this story is the gun. In a famous interview, the Police Commissioner Giuttari declared that he believed there still was a lot to say about that gun. What are thoughts on his declaration? Are you convinced that the same gun was used in the 1968 murder? Some have even hypothesized that two different guns were simultaneously used in some the crimes based on the number of shells found on the crime scenes. Any thoughts?

I definitely believe that there was only one gun. It is highly probable that it was the same gun registered to Agresti, a Sardinian immigrant from Villacidro and that later went missing. The analyses at that time made it clear all the marks on the exploded shells were identical! The ammunitions came from 2 different boxes: one with copper-lead head bullets and one with regular bullets. There are no facts or clues that could lead us to believe that there were two shooters. Furthermore, the Beretta caliber 22 models 70, 72, or 74 can hold up to 10 rounds.

In your opinion, how was the whole Spalleti affair handled? What could he have possibly witnessed? His behavior over the years has been questionable: from what it seems, he has never received large sums of money in exchange for his silence given that his lifestyle remained the same. What could have then been the reason for his silence? The fact that he could have been prosecuted due to his involvement in some serious crime (perhaps he assisted the Monster) or was it just that he was scared?

I believe that Spalleti did see something the night of the murder in Arrigo Avenue. However, I think arresting him was a mistake because had he been released and then under surveillance, we could have gotten more information. His silence was probably due to him being scared all the more so his brother received a phone call during which threats were made towards Spalleti himself. This is one of the many obscure aspects of the event.

We have have always been convinced that somewhere in the world of peeping toms, there could be another Spalletti who could have seen or heard something but who did not come forward for fear of ending up in Spalletti's shoes. What is your take on this?

I agree that it is impossible that nobody saw anything given that the crime areas in those days were heavily frequented by peeping toms. In my opinion, the Monster would scour the area and then he would "clear it" so to say of potential intruders. There were at least two cases of peeping toms mysteriously killed reported in the news. And then, there is Fosco Fabbri's testimony in which he declares having been verbally abused and threatened with a gun by a uniformed man as related by the lawyer Nino Filastò in a recent interview.

How would you say the Monster selected his victims?

I believe he mainly selected the locations although it is a possibility that he meticulously studied the habits and daily routines of the couples prior to striking. We must remember that in the 70s/80s, the act of love making in a car, particularly in small towns, was considered extremely transgressive. For that reason, the couples had to find very isolated and obscure areas that would otherwise have been unfamiliar to them.

Following the French couple's murder, the Monster mails the famous letter containing a strip of Nadine Mauriot's breast to the attention of prosecutor Silvia Della Monica. The envelope was mailed many kilometers away from the crime scene. Do you think that the Monster drove all that distance the night of the murder? How could he be so sure that he would not have been pulled over for a routine police control?

Well, we are once again speculating. He could have mailed the envelope the following day or perhaps that same night with the help of an accomplice... It is certain that the act was premeditated. I think that the envelope was prepared prior to the murder which I believe was committed on Saturday, not on Sunday. The Monster deliberately chose a couple of foreigners in an attempt to delay the discovery of the bodies. This way, the envelope could reach its destination and create general panic prior to the bodies being found. The choice of the town where the letter was mailed from, San Piero a Sieve, has for the Monster, a specific meaning: one that is not easy to decode, but nonetheless specific.

What is your interpretation of the letter years later? What is your take on the spelling error on the envelope (the word "republica" written with one b)? Does it indicate the Monster's poor educational background or was it just astute diversion attempt?

Out of the many anonymous letters mailed during that time, the one addressed to Prosecutor Della Monica is the only one that was surely sent by the Monster. I find it hard to believe that the famous missing letter "b" was some sort of an encrypted message... I would think that it was simply a spelling error.

Let's talk about the cases of red-herring: the anonymous letters in this story are discarded ,as in so many other criminal cases in Italy. Do you believe that these letters were viewed as red-herring or that they could have been from someone who knew something and was trying to communicate with the investigators to clear their conscience? Or perhaps the investigators hid behind the "anonymous letter" tactic to justify some unorthodox operations.

We would need access to the millions of anonymous letters that were received in those years in order to respond to this question... it is possible that some of the letters contained valid information that went under the radar! We can certainly say that none of these letters contained any information that led to the identification of the Monster. The anonymous letter suggesting that Pacciani should be investigated only two days following the last double homicide could have been important!

However, the its author did not go further than describe Pacciani as a diabolical and violent man without providing any substantial clue that could have been useful for the investigation.It would be interesting to know if a comparative calligraphic examination of the accusatory letters towards Pacciani and all the other anonymous letters mailed to the police has ever been performed. It is undeniable that there were a few cases of red-herring to throw off the investigation! I personally believe that the letter with the newspaper article that indicated the Sardinian lead shortly following the Montespertoli murder of 1982 is a perfect example of red-herring by the Monster.

Since 1985, the Monster has officially stopped killing. What made him stop? Could he have decided to alter his methods in an effort to stay away from the media so he would not be identified? It is a fact that serial killers of this caliber are usually unable to stop killing unless driven by an external factor.

Maybe he died shortly after the last homicide. It is also possible that could have changed his ways and his targets. Let me remind you that during those years in Florence, there were many unsolved brutal killings of prostitutes, about eight if I remember. And then, there were other murders just as worrisome in the early 90s that were certainly linked to the affair of the Monster. An example is the murder of Francesco Vinci, his shepherd Angelo Vargiu and his lover Milva Malatesta.

In our book, we offer an alternative reconstruction of the Baccaiano murder. We basically claim that the Monster was behind the wheel of Paolo Mainardi's car which ended up in the ditch in an attempt to move the car away from the emplacement that was too close to the main road. What do you think about our reconstruction?

I think that theory is partially true in the sense that based on the version given by the paramedics, it seems that Mainardi was in the back seat. However, it is also true traces of Mainardi's blood was found in the middle of the road as revealed by the crime scene photos. This could also lead to believe that Mainardi was initially shot while he was on the driver's side prior to being moved to the back seat. This reconstruction would explain the shattered back window and the position of the shooting location.

Lets' say that the killer is that same that committed that 1968 murder, why would there be such a long break between the first 2 murders?

Although the 1968 murder was allegedly committed by Stefano Mele, there is still a 7 year gap between the 1974 murder and that of 1981. That could have been due to a convenient "evolution" of the Monster. The killer could possibly have been away or been in situations that prevented him from executing the killings. Perhaps the impulse to kill was derived from a demented escalation alimented by the world's interest in his terrifying ventures.

Was the Germans' murder a mistake as so many claim?

The impression is that unlike the other murders, this one was executed in a hurry...the killer did not complete any action beyond shooting his gun! Let's remember that the Monster always stabs the man t ensure his death but in this case, he made no use of the knife. He shoots and then, he walks away.

Do you think that Monster is Tuscan?

I don't know! He was definitely familiar with the area and was very comfortable moving around in the dark.

Had you been heading the investigations, which alternate leads would you have followed?

The 2001 investigations (the Narducci lead TN) seemed to take the right direction and could have hatched better results than the other investigations but they took off too late.

I do not believe in a completely secluded "monster" from an aristocratic background. Although I think that he did the killings by himself, I am also certain he had the help and complicity of someone on the outside. The maniac group murder plot seems improbable from a criminology standpoint. Filastò's theory has some merits but I have a hard time picturing the Monster on a killing spree with the police lights mounted on his car.

What do you think of the Spezi theory? Why didn't the person identified as possibly being the Monster of Florence speak up publicly? In the English version of the book, the person suspected of being the Monster is clearly nominated. I am looking at page 194 of the American version of the book where I can find the entire account of the interview given by the person who, according to Spezi & Preston's reconstruction, could be a candidate for the title of Monster. His first and last name are explicitly stated here but not in the Italian version of the book. Why has there never been any action against that person?

I don't have an answer as to why this person has remained silent. However, Spezi & Preston's hypothesis is interesting although it needs to be examined more in depth. The investigators would certainly be in a position to objectively evaluate the theory by comparing it to their findings. One of the facts that make the story of the Monster of Florence so captivating is that everybody can come up with a different scenario. There is also a missing element in all the suggested theories... The last piece of the puzzle.

Pacciani is one of the most unsettling characters in the story of the Monster: what do you think of Paccani and the pick-nicking friends? Do you think that Lotti's claims are credible?

Personally, I do not think that Lotti's declarations are reliable. I feel that Pacciani might have had a marginal role in the event and that he ended paying for everyone. As for Vanni, I think that he played no role in it at all. These are obviously personal convictions. Let's remember that some of the verdicts indicate that the pick-nicking friends were the perpetrators of the last four double homicides. The principal suspects were acquitted "because the fact was without foundation". That is the umpteenth anomaly of an incredible event which could not have been written by the world's greatest "crime novelist".

Paolo Cochi at the 2011 Sugarpulp Festival.

INTERVIEW
WITH STEFANO NAZZI

Stefano Nazzi is one of the most important voices in Italian true-crime podcasting. With INDAGINI, Nazzi carved out a place for himself thanks to decades of work in the field and a style that leaves little room for narrative flourishes and a lot of room for facts. That approach turned him into a cultural phenomenon loved by a huge Italian audience.

We met Stefano Nazzi backstage at the PalaGeox in Padua, minutes before a stop on his theatre tour INDAGINI LIVE dedicated to the Monster of Florence. The show was sold out, the venue filled with thousands of people ready to relive one of the darkest stories in Italian crime history. Despite the preparations and the tension before stepping on stage, Nazzi welcomed us with complete openness. With him we talked about the case, its complexities, and the way it still splits public opinion.

Stefano, you arrive at the Monster of Florence case after years of work in true crime. Many describe it as the most difficult, the most tangled, almost mythological. Why did you wait so long before tackling it?

I waited because I wanted to study everything I possibly could. Once you step into the Monster's crimes, you realise the case is layered with superstructures, baseless assumptions, and theories that are pure fantasy criminology. If you stick to the objective data, there is a judicial truth and a handful of plausible hypotheses, like those connected to Lake Trasimeno or other potential perpetrators. But most reconstructions have no concrete foundation.

It's a case that deeply divides the public. Few crime stories in Italy are known in such detail by so many people. How do you deal with audiences that arrive with completely different backgrounds?

It's true. Some people know every single detail, others have only heard about the case, and there's an entire generation that doesn't know it at all. I try to keep my distance and stick to concrete, judicial elements. That lets me speak to the die-hard enthusiasts who have read everything and also to younger listeners who approach the case for the first time.

There is a judicial truth, but not a shared historical truth. Do you think we'll ever get there?

I don't think so. In Italy, reopening a trial requires new and solid evidence, and at the moment none exists. The recent exhumation of Vinci's body, for example, led nowhere. The case stays divided. There are those who believe in a higher level, those who focus only on the "compagni di merende" and Pacciani, and those who imagine completely different scenarios. The fact is that the objective elements are few, so many hypotheses survive, including the most imaginative ones.

Do you think the perception of this case changes depending on where you are in Italy?

Absolutely. In Tuscany it is still an open wound. People there feel the Monster on their skin. In Umbria the discussion intertwines with the Narducci case. In other regions there's less direct involvement. Many people in my audiences tell me they never really knew this story. It's surprising, because we're talking about the most notorious Italian serial killer along with Donato Bilancia. With the difference that, while we know everything about Bilancia, the Monster of Florence is still surrounded by a massive halo of mystery.

Let's talk about evidence and trials. Many feel those trials were more spectacle than substance. Do you agree?

Yes. They were spectacular trials, widely covered by the media, but with very little substantial evidence. The verdicts identified guilty parties, but they didn't erase the doubts. Even today the case is still full of shadows.

One last question. You're used to working with a podcast, alone in front of a microphone. What changes when you find yourself on a stage in front of thousands of people?

Everything changes. Speaking alone into a microphone is one thing. Standing in front of two thousand people is another. You need to hold their attention and avoid boring them or distracting them. It's a long story, full of developments, and keeping it alive in front of a crowd is a huge challenge. But when you succeed, the emotion is incredible.

Giacomo Brunoro, Stefano Nazzi and Jacopo
Pezzan.

INTERVIEW
WITH FRANCIS TRINIPET

For the final appendix of our book, we spoke with one of the most well-known and followed "mostrologi": Professor Francesco Petrini, known online as Francis Trinipet. A historian and university professor, Petrini has become a reference point for enthusiasts thanks to his "zero-budget films" published on his YouTube channel, all dedicated to the Monster of Florence case, marked by a creative style and a strong poetic impulse. A firm supporter of the so-called judicial truth, Petrini believes that Pietro Pacciani was the Monster and that he acted alongside the compagni di merende, but under the control of a second level, most likely of an esoteric nature. We interviewed him on our podcast True Crime Diaries to explore his point of view on the case and on the relationship between judicial truth and historical truth.

Francis, let's start from the basics. Why, in your opinion, does the Monster of Florence case still divide people so deeply today?

Because it's a case that was born with plenty of anomalies. On one hand, we have a clear judicial truth: the compagni di merende were convicted for some of the murders and, legally speaking, the Monster has been identified. On the other hand, there are gaps, mysteries, grey areas that open the door to endless interpretations. When the evidence is scarce and inconclusive, it's inevitable that a fertile ground for hypotheses and fantasies emerges.

You're among those who strongly defend the judicial truth. Why?

Because, beyond the many alternative theories, it's the only framework that held up in a courtroom. It's not perfect, of course, but it outlines a plausible dynamic. Pietro Pacciani wasn't a refined intellectual. He was a farmer with a violent past and a brutal temperament. Beside him, Mario Vanni and Giancarlo Lotti, two marginal figures capable of anything either to please someone or to gain a few crumbs of power. It's the picture of a degraded humanity that fits the way the murders were committed.

But then how do you explain the murders before 1982, the ones not covered by the final convictions?

That's where the so-called "second level" comes in. I don't believe in a Pacciani who suddenly turns into a serial killer on his own. I believe he and his companions were used. Crude tools, easy to control for those who, behind the scenes, had greater interests and motivations. The execution methods, the ritual of the excisions, certain details that point to a precise symbolism. These are elements that suggest a higher level, probably connected to esoteric practices.

Many observers find it difficult to reconcile Pacciani's roughness with a "cultured" or esoteric context.

That's exactly the point. Pacciani isn't the mastermind. Pacciani is the executor. His role is the arm, not the mind. He is the perfect man to use: violent, unscrupulous, inclined to obey if guided in the right way. And around him there were other figures, other presences capable of pulling the strings. That's what I mean when I talk about a second level. A dark direction, able to exploit men like him for purposes that go beyond a simple sexual murder.

In your YouTube videos you give the reconstruction an almost poetic tone. Why this choice?

Because the Monster case isn't only judicial history. It's a story that marked Italy. It shaped the national imagination, terrified entire generations, brought ancient fears back to the surface. Telling it only as a legal file means diminishing it. I want to make people understand that behind every detail, every document, there are lives, stories, pain. Creativity and poetic language help remind us that we're not talking only about papers, but about human beings.

Do you think we will ever reach a shared historical truth?

No. Every school of thought is now deeply rooted. There are those who believe in the Sardinian trail, those who believe in the policeman trail, those who believe in a single unidentified serial killer. And then there are the supporters of the judicial truth, like me. No one will ever convince the others. What we can do is try to piece things together honestly, without pushing too far. Historical truth in a case like this remains elusive. But judicial truth, with all its limits, is the fixed point we must accept.

To close, what do you think is the greatest legacy of the Monster case?

The legacy is twofold. On one hand, it leaves us with the bitter lesson of an investigative system that, in the crucial years, wasn't ready to handle a phenomenon of this scale. On the other hand, it shows how the fascination with evil still today generates stories, studies, artistic works. It's a case that will never stop sparking debate because it touches deep chords in our society: the relationship with violence, fear of the other, the allure of mystery.

Giacomo Brunoro, Francis Trinipet, and Jacopo Pezzan. Photo taken at the Italian Conference on the Monster of Florence Case, organized by Angelo Marotta in collaboration with LA CASE Books.

THE END…?

Jacopo Pezzan and Giacomo Bruoro at VENICE NOIR Festival, 2025.

JACOPO PEZZAN
& GIACOMO BRUNORO

Both from Padua, Pezzan and Brunoro met in the early 1990s. They have explored Italian mysteries, Vatican murders, the dark stories of serial killers, and some of the most famous crime cases tied to contemporary pop icons in a successful series of books and audiobooks. Their podcast, TRUE CRIME DIARIES, is available on all major digital platforms.

LA CASE BOOKS

LA CASE Books was founded in Los Angeles in 2010 as an editorial project between Italy and the United States. From the beginning, LA CASE Books operated on the digital market: "great stories at a small price" is our philosophy.

LA CASE Books is one of the first publishing companies in the world that produced and sold ebooks and audiobooks specifically made and designed for digital readers. The length of our texts, our style and the choice of the subjects make them perfect products for the most modern readers. An international team that works (and has fun!) everywhere.

At the beginning of 2010 Pezzan, who had moved to Los Angeles, understood that the digital is disruptive to publishing market. So when in Italy it was not possible to buy ebooks on iTunes, and Kindle Store was active only in the United States, LA CASE Books began to publish ebooks and audiobooks in Italian and English on the international market.

In 2020, to celebrate the first ten years of the publishing house, they also began releasing print editions.

Today LA CASE Books has a catalog of more than 2,000 titles, including print books, ebooks, podcasts, audiobooks, and documentaries in English, Italian, German, French, Spanish, Russian, Polish, and Portuguese. The company is present on all major international digital stores.

www.lacasebooks.com